OLD HILARITY

BY

A. J. G. PRIEST

Professor of Law,
University of Virginia

THE MICHIE COMPANY
Law Publishers
Charlottesville, Va.

Copyright 1965
by
The Michie Company

DEDICATION

For the late Joel L. Priest of Boise, Idaho, and Henderson, Kentucky, wit, raconteur, rare spirit; and for C. Hamilton Moses of Little Rock, Arkansas, and Clem B. Holding of Raleigh, North Carolina, who greatly have received, and generously poured forth, God's good, rich gift of laughter.

A. J. G. P.

INTRODUCTION

I am a veteran of World War I and therefore no longer a boy. And I am a collector. I gather stories.

I have been at my self-assignment for more than 60 years, as I could not have been older than six when my father told me the first anecdote I can recall. It was brief: Teacher, "Give me a sentence using the words 'bitter end.'" Henry, "The cat ran under the bed. The dog ran after her and bitter end."

Not belly-shaking in this sixth decade of the twentieth century, but it was perfectly tailored to its audience. I was convulsed. The recollection touches my risibilities lightly even at the moment.

Progress has been made. My memory is retentive and, through the years, I have assembled anecdotes from every part of the land: Idaho, New York, Virginia, Utah, California, Texas, the District of Columbia, North and South Carolina, the Province of Ontario, Massachusetts, Colorado and many way-stations. There has been only one criterion. Was I amused?

The bringing together of this collection has given me personal satisfaction and sundry ventral areas have been wholesomely exercised as the tales have been told. The world may not be panting for them in book form, but the hour *is* grim. Humor is needed.

Aubrey Mennen's brilliant retelling of that vivid Hindu epic, "The Ramayana," states the case for humor. This final question is put by Prince Rama to Valmiki, who has been his tutor, philosopher and friend, "In this world of illusion, is there anything you believe in as real?" "Certainly," Valmiki replies, "Three things: God, human folly and laughter. Since the first two pass our comprehension, we must do what we can with the third."

Consider the computer. Even if properly fed all the more engaging humor from Joe Miller through Mark Twain to Bennett Cerf, such a device could hardly be expected to make the hills ring with hilarity. Wit plainly would be beyond it. Only a man, equipped with mind *and* emotions, can laugh.

There have been many omissions. No Johnson stories. No Kennedy stories. No Goldwater stories. No Eisenhower stories. No Roosevelt stories. No stereotyping. No yarns aimed at Negroes, Jews, Irishmen, Scots, Germans, or any other minority group. Nothing from Hollywood, Broadway or Madison Avenue. No perversion. No homosexual tripe. Not a single mother-in-law gag; they usually aren't funny anyhow.

But situation humor, of course. And word play. Some vulgarity. J. B. Thomas of Fort Worth insists that the basic predicate of all humor is vulgarity. I think he's wrong, but he states a persuasive case. In all events, my collection does include humor that arises (a) from dealing with pain playfully (Max Eastman's definition) and (b) from incongruity in many of its manifestations.

Some of the stories are new. Several, but not many, of the more venerable specimens may have been published. England makes a few contributions, but the tales are largely Americana. Only one friend under 60 has been quoted. This is pre-atomic humor; it is fun-making from years when we were less exacerbated.

The stories have been written substantially as they were told. Four-letter words appear occasionally. I have used in context that too-characteristic American locution which attributes canine maternity to the object of one's epithet. But I doubt that I shall contribute to juvenile or even ministerial delinquency.

By and large, the episodes recounted actually happened or might have happened without straining the imagination too severely. Ornamentation has been used for verisimilitude's sake, but sparingly. Most of the names are genuine; only targets or victims have received fictional designations.

So that I may bow out after this introduction, the tales are told by my late cousin, A. Janxton Gussman, who also was a collector of such trifles and who would be glad to act as narrator if he were still around.

When A. H. Upham, then president of Miami

University, gave me a copy of his readable and scholarly history, "Old Miami," he inscribed it, "For A.J.G.P. Some of this is true." I can apply his characterization to this volume.

I have been privileged to listen to great raconteurs. The first among them was my father, the late Joel L. Priest of Boise, Idaho, favorite toastmaster of the Rocky Mountain area, wit, lover of humor. Second by only a narrow margin is C. Hamilton Moses of Little Rock, Arkansas, who often is as eloquent as he can be hilarious, and whose half-telling of seven or eight consecutive stories, followed by the picking up of their several punch lines, is an extraordinary *tour de force*. Clem B. Holding of Raleigh, North Carolina, whose smile is one of America's most infectious, ranks third by a mere half-length.

There have been numerous others, many of them now swapping yarns around a camp fire in the Elysian Fields: John Corette, Frank Kerr and Frank W. Bird of Montana; George M. Gadsby of Salt Lake City, Utah; J. M. B. Hoxsey of Athens, Georgia, and New York City; Claude Sapp of Columbia, South Carolina; Bill Dawson of Cleveland, Ohio; Lou Merwin of Portland, Oregon; Percy Corbett of Princeton, New Jersey; J. B. Thomas of Fort Worth, Texas; John S. Wise of Allentown, Pennsylvania; Allan A. Smith of Portland, Oregon; Cyril F. H. Carson of Toronto, Canada; John S. Battle, Sr., Hardy C. Dillard, T. Munford Boyd, George Gilmer, Charles O. Gregory and Charles Bunn of Charlottesville, Virginia; Chester Poole of Ivy, Virginia; T. Justin Moore of Richmond, Virginia; Joel L. Priest, Jr., of Salt Lake City, Utah, and many more—some casual acquaintances; some friends of friends—who have induced deep, belly laughter and brightened the land for a moment. To the living among them—retirement age or more with few exceptions—I voice gratitude and admiration. To those of you who are no longer with us, I lift a glass that brims with warm affection. The planet is a grayer place without you.

A. J. G. PRIEST
Charlottesville, Virginia

TABLE OF CONTENTS

	PAGE
Introduction	5
Politics! Congress!	13
Sports in Some Variety	29
Academe, Shades of	47
Lawyers and Judges	56
Accounting—But Briefly	94
Religion and Humor	96
Raconteur Extraordinary	106
Here a Hodge, There a Podge	121
The Fourth Estate	149
Public Utilities: Their Feeding and Care	153
The Great Empty Spaces	168
The Medical Fraternity	179
Pre-epilogue and Ep.	185
The Decalogue of the Humorous Anecdote	187

POLITICS! CONGRESS!

Politics is a battered occupation. Its practitioners are frequently given to demagogy. They tend to be portentous. They have small acquaintance with humility. Yet they love laughter. As a rule, however, they bow at Comus's shrine in private. The dear people vote for Old Sobersides. That warm smile—former President Eisenhower's, for example—wins friends, but a candidate's too-ready apprehension of humor has often been suspect. The radical right would never have countenanced anything but intense seriousness from Senator Goldwater. Whether he was capable of anything else is, of course, quite another question.

The late President Kennedy's flashing sallies at his press conferences should have delighted even Mississippians. He was informed by wit, gaiety, an upwelling sense of humor—qualities which helped courage and intelligence to mould his greatness. Humor probably sustained him more generously than any of his predecessors save Abraham Lincoln, with whom he now stands.

President Johnson's humor is quick, genial, robust and generous. Furthermore, he tells a story well. His audiences will increasingly appreciate him. And they should.

Knee unhinged; tongue a razor

Senator William E. Borah of Idaho assured me, just a few months before his death, that this was the most crushing bit of repartee he had heard in his 30 years in the Senate:

Senator Furnifold Simmons of North Carolina was delivering an address on the Senate floor when Senator John Sharp Williams of Mississippi came wavering down the aisle, clutching at desks as he proceeded.

Simmons was an ardent prohibitionist. Williams was not. And the two cordially disliked each other. Observing John Sharp's apparent condition and not realizing that alcohol unhinged the Mississipian's knees long before it dulled the razor-edge of his mind, Simmons said, "I would like to observe, Mr. President, that whenever I address the Senate of the United States, I am always in full possession of my faculties."

John Sharp was a little deaf and he asked quickly, "What was that?"

Simmons replied, "I would like to say, suh, for your particular benefit, suh, that whenever I address the Senate of the United States, I am always in full possession of my faculties."

John Sharp snorted. "Huh," he said, "what good does that do you?"

Heflin the dextrous

Tom Heflin of Alabama, who served for many years in both the House and the Senate, made a career of hating and fearing the "Pope of Rome." His attacks were slanderous, demagogic and reckless. But he was an amiable enough person and, after one of his diatribes, Pat Daugherty, who represented a Philadelphia district, took him aside. "Tom," he said, "don't you realize that the great strength of the Democratic party is in the big cities and that the Irish Catholic vote is usually controlling in those cities? Every time you make one of your hate-the-Catholics speeches, you alienate hundreds of Irish votes. You are doing a serious and dangerous disservice to the party."

"Why, my dear Pat," Tom replied, "you gravely misunderstand and misapprehend me. I don't hate the Irish Catholics. I *love* the Irish Catholics. It's them damn' *Roman* Catholics I'm after!"

Pilgrimage

Henry S. Bannon of Portsmouth, Ohio, served in the House of Representatives through Theodore Roosevelt's full term. He was friendly with Tom Heflin and was awakened early one morning to be told that Tom was about to be arraigned and might need a character witness.

The Alabaman had thought that a Washington citizen failed to yield his streetcar seat to a young woman with sufficient alacrity, had pushed him through a window and had then winged him with a pocket derringer as he fled up Pennsylvania Avenue.

Bannon was at the arraignment as a matter of course. He later offered this as a substantially accurate transcript of the testimony of one of Heflin's Alabama colleagues:

"You and Congressman Heflin were together yesterday afternoon?"

"Yes, suh."

"Please tell us in your own words exactly what happened while you were in his company."

"Well, suh, Congressman Heflin and I left the halls of Congress together about four o'clock yesterday afternoon and we repaired to the Raleigh hotel."

"What did you do?"

"We entered the bar at the Raleigh and we had two whisky sours, suh."

"Then what did you do?"

"We proceeded to the Willard hotel and again entered the bar. In that case, we had two mo' whisky sours, suh."

"Please go on."

"We continued our course, this time stopping at the Washington hotel. The whisky sours served at the Washington bar are especially palatable, so we each had three of them, suh."

"Then what happened?"

"Congressman Heflin looked at his watch and he said, 'Mah God, I'll be late for mah temperance lecture at the First Methodist Church.' Then he boarded that streetcar and the unfortunate episode transpired, suh!"

He reported what he saw

The doorkeeper for the House of Representatives in one of Idaho's territorial years was addicted to the spirituous rather than the spiritual. And the Governor's secretary was six feet eight inches tall, his personal architecture that of a lathe.

This particular afternoon, the Governor's secretary came to the House, shook the doorkeeper into consciousness, and said, "I have a message from the Governor. Go tell the Speaker there is a message from the Governor."

The doorkeeper bleared up at the secretary's towering height, got to his feet and staggered down the aisle. "Mr. Speaker," he announced, "Mr. Speaker! Message from the Governor! Message from the Governor! Just been brought in by a son-of-a-bitch on horseback!"

OH—2

Cabal in Salt Lake City

Fisher Harris, an early secretary of Salt Lake City's chamber of commerce, was from Virginia, son of a Confederate major, and passionately devoted to the Lost Cause. He rarely made a public address in which he did not refer throbbingly to "the great, white arms of the Confederacy."

Republicans had predominated in Utah, but when the Populist-Democratic movement rolled over the far West, Harris had casually accepted the nomination for County Recorder on that ticket. Swept into office, he continued to give himself exclusively to his duties as secretary of the chamber of commerce.

Then when election time rolled around in another two years, several of his Democratic friends came to him and reported unkind local gossip to the effect that the only time he ever went to his office in the county court house was for the purpose of picking up his monthly check.

"That, suh," Fisher replied warmly, "is an infamous and outrageous cabal. I always have my check sent up to me, suh!"

Politics intrafamilial

In the 1880's, Senator James Mourmount of Utah's Lee County, a Republican, was opposed for election by his third wife, Sophia, an ardent Democrat.

When Sophia met reporters, she said, "Now, boys, be sure to refer to me as Senator Mourmount's second plural wife. That is the only correct designation."

Sophia won and a too-short-lived Salt Lake City weekly commented, "Bedfellows make strange politics!"

Grandmother in the pokey

Much more recently, a committee of the Utah legislature held hearings on a proposed blue law that would have sealed the State hermetically on First Day. Advocates of the measure were making progress until a Salt Lake lawyer appeared, "Look, boys," he said. "I work on Sunday, and you say I can't. I have to. Just how would you feel if your dear old grandmother got all gowed up Saturday night and made the pokey, but I couldn't swing her cell door until noon on Monday? Think about it!"

Unfavorable committee report.

Life's span is tenuous

In the earlier years of this century, the favorite gathering place of north Idaho's Democratic political leaders was the old Spokane Hotel, in Spokane, Washington. Chief among those gentry was Peter Brown, whose major weakness was conviviality and who was discovered by Charlie Arney in the hotel lobby at ten o'clock on a May morning. Pete's gregariousness the night before had been ardent and he sat groaning, with his head between his hands.

"Look, my friend," said Charlie, "don't you think you need a touch of the hair of the dog who sank his teeth into you last night?"

"No!", Pete replied. "Never again. I'm through. I'm not going to take another drink as long as I live."

At five o'clock that afternoon, Arney found Pete in the bar, recovered, jovial, genially lubricated.

"Come, come, Pete," Charlie objected, "I thought you told me this morning that you were never going to take another drink as long as you lived."

"I did say that," Pete announced. "I did say that. But listen, you son-of-a-bitch, I didn't expect to live this long!"

Mine pit to the Senate; no way-station

A United States Senator, who shall be nameless, went from mucker to millionaire in a brief while, and he remained a genial, rough-cut stone long after the legislature of his western State sent him to Washington.

The cultured and cultivated Senator Hoar of Massachusetts was intrigued by the miner-statesman and became his good friend. That is, until they encountered each other on the Senate floor as a session was about to begin and the westerner greeted his colleague with, "Ah, there, Senator. How is Mrs. W. this morning?"

Do you monog?

Reed Smoot, one of the early United States Senators from Utah, was never a polygamist but he came under unjust attack from partisans who questioned his qualifications for political purposes. There was much argument until Boies Penrose of Pennsylvania, a bachelor and a gay blade, got the floor.

"Mr. President," he said, "the Senator from Utah has never been a polygamist but, even assuming that he had been, I do not believe that the soaring morals of this august body would be too gravely impaired by the presence among us of a polygamist who no longer polygs, sitting with monogamists who do not monog!"

Slayden could pick 'em

Shortly after World War I, when anti-German feeling still ran high, Congressman James L. Slaydeñ decided to appoint to the Naval Academy an attractive young man from a wholly German community north of San Antonio. His friends urged that the appointment would be unpopular and unwise; that it plainly was bad politics. But Jim Slaydeñ said, "No! I'm going through with it. This youngster has all the qualifications: intelligence, personality, loyalty. He'll be a good, average naval officer, maybe better than the average."

The experiment was not unsuccessful. Chester Nimitz proved to be a satisfactory midshipman.

Not perspiration: sweat

Wayman Pranson, highly regarded but unsuccessful candidate for the Republican gubernatorial nomination in Idaho fifty years ago, was fastidious as to personal appearance far beyond the custom of his time. He dressed in white, shaved twice a day, used a special bay rum, insisted upon a bath-equipped hotel room. His intelligence and ability were recognized, but he failed to appeal to a party convention largely made up of delegates who sweated and were not concerned when or whether others became aware of their exudations.

After the convention, Joel Priest, then a newspaperman, asked Wayman to explain his defeat. "Put it this way, Joel," he said. "I guess the proletariat just can't stand the smell of the soap!"

They were earnest in Kentucky

In Kentucky a decade earlier, another party convention denied nomination, again for the governorship, to a candidate who had been favored for eighteen months. That gentleman was neither Kentucky's nor the South's best loser. In fact, he refused to permit the nomination to be made unanimous and demanded the privilege of the floor.

"Mr. Chairman," he said, "I trust that I shall never again be so unfortunate as to seek the suffrage of my fellow Democrats at a state convention of our glorious party. But if I do, I shall know better how to appeal to the hearts of the Louisville delegation!" And he shook a silver dollar at them.

They came boiling over the benches. No party convention in Kentucky's turbulent political history produced more black eyes or broken noses.

Loyalty has limits

In another party convention of the same Kentucky period, Bantrud Breckridge, also a gubernatorial aspirant, lost after having declared on the floor, "Why, my dear friends, I would vote for a yellow dog if such an animal received the nomination of the inspired party of Grover Cleveland, Thomas Jefferson and Jefferson Davis."

In the November election, however, Bantrud campaigned actively and effectively for the Republican candidate. Friends came to him. "Ban," said one of them, "I thought you said that you would vote for a yellow dog if he were nominated on the Democratic ticket."

"Such was my statement, suh," said Ban. "Such *was* my statement. But further than that, suh, by God, suh, you shall not force me, suh."

Memory's frailties

Secretary of Commerce Luther R. Hodges tells about one of his predecessors as Governor of North Carolina, call him Ham Getteson, who was greeting a long line of constituents after one of his addresses: "How are you, old boy? How's the family? Delighted to see *you* here, Pete. Yes, the weather has been good to us! Thank *you* for coming to listen." And much more.

Then arrived the inevitable nuisance who clasped Ham's hand in an iron grip and said, "Ham, you don't know mah name. Come on, Ham, tell me mah name. You can't tell me mah name!"

Ham tried hard to pull the gentleman along, but failed to budge him either by force or with explanations. The line stopped cold and Ham turned to one of his staff, "Bill, will somebody please tell this son-of-a-bitch what his name is? He's forgotten and he's trying to find it out from me!"

Mores

In that hectic and unhappy period of Congressional history, 1865 to 1870, a young man from Nevada was named an assistant clerk in the United States Senate through the good offices of William M. Stewart, elected in 1863 as Nevada's first Senator.

The young man had referred to Senator Sumner of Massachusetts, in the presence of witnesses, as "a puritannical son-of-a-bitch." That remark soon reached Senator Sumner's outraged ear and he immediately sought the young clerk's job.

The desperate clerk invoked the aid of his sponsor and Senator Stewart approached Senator Sumner for purposes of placation:

"My dear Senator, I would have you know that the term 'son-of-a-bitch' does not connote in Nevada all that it does in Massachusetts.

"For example, my dear Senator, I come home and one of my constituents claps me on the back and exclaims, 'Welcome back, Bill, you old son-of-a-bitch', I know he's my friend. However, my dear Senator, when a constituent says to me, 'How do you do, Senator?', I quickly turn to my secretary and tell him, 'Look out for that son-of-a-bitch—he's getting cold.' "

The response parliamentary

On a visit to the University of Virginia, the Earl of Kilmuir, then Lord High Chancellor of Great Britain, related that he had become hopelessly lost while motoring through Devon. He had stopped in despair and, when a native appeared, he asked, "Where am I?"

"Why, you be in a motor car," was the reply.

Some months had elapsed, so that Lord Kilmuir was able to comment dispassionately, "That really was the perfect parliamentary response. It was terse. It was relevant. It was truthful. And it imparted no jot or tittle of information."

You can count on your friends

Judge William M. Morgan was first elected to the Idaho Supreme Court in a day when northern Idaho held itself sharply aloof from southern Idaho, politically and sentimentally. Morgan, who came from Moscow in the north, was asked for the basic principle on which he would campaign. "Quite elementary," he said, "I shall appeal to the prejudice of the north and to the enlightened fair-mindedness of the south." His victory was overwhelming.

Vox populi

No fewer than 40 years ago, the late Chief Justice Charles A. O'Niell of the Louisiana Supreme Court was the principal guest at a New Orleans dinner given in an apartment happily located above Antoine's, then and still a significant gathering place for gourmets. After coffee, our host said, "Judge, why don't you tell Gussman how you were elected to the Supreme Court for the first time?"

"Well, young man," the Chief Justice began, "this is how it happened: All of the candidates for Democratic nomination to the Court were scheduled to appear before a mass meeting to be held in New Orleans. That was fair enough, but I was from outside Orleans parish. Furthermore, I was one of ten candidates and I was afraid the presiding officer wouldn't call on me.

"About twenty minutes before the meeting began, I mingled in the crowd and picked out a brass-voiced gentleman who plainly had drunk earnestly enough to dissipate all his inhibitions. 'My friend,' I said, 'You should see to it that Charlie O'Niell gets a chance to speak. He is eloquent, persuasive, powerful, highly intelligent. It clearly is in the best interests of all concerned that he should address the crowd.'

"One of the candidates from New Orleans was introduced, but he had spoken for no more than ten minutes when my friend began to yell 'We want O'Niell.' And he persisted so vigorously that the chairman, yielding to popular opinion, presented me as the second speaker.

"But my ally continued to shout, 'We want O'Niell' and the chairman observed, 'But I have given you Mr. O'Niell, my good friend. This is Mr. O'Niell speaking!'

"'Hell', was his rejoinder, 'that ain't O'Niell. That's the son-of-a-bitch who told me to holler!'

"Just for the record, son, I was elected by 36 votes. And I expect to stay on the bench as long as I live."

SPORTS IN SOME VARIETY

The engaging, informed and articulate masters of their craft who have written and who write sports columns—Grantland Rice, W. O. McGeahan, Red Smith, John Kieran, Arthur Daley, Joe Williams and Frank Graham of New York; Charles Dryden of Chicago; Shirley Povich of Washington, D. C.; L. H. Gregory of Portland, Oregon; Curly Grieve of San Francisco, and many others—have made significant items of humor within their sphere as rare as Mycenaean masks of gold. These few samples may have escaped their attention.

BASEBALL

The Babe had a predecessor

Joel Priest heard this expression of serene confidence—outdone only by Babe Ruth's pointed bat of forty years later—in 1893. This also happened in Chicago.

That city's fabulous White Stockings were playing the original Baltimore Orioles: last half of the ninth, score tied, two out, a fast man on third, Pop Anson at the plate.

The base runner took a dangerously long lead, drew one throw, then another and another. Pop

Anson finally became annoyed. He glared down the foul line and advised ringingly, "Hold your base, kid. I'll shor' hit 'er!"

He did. But naturally.

Chivs and beauty

Charlie Dryden must have passed from all but a few clinging memories. This Dryden sentence should, I submit, be preserved: "All the beauty and chivalry of Chicago were there: ten thousand chivs and five thousand beauts."

Not even Ty Cobb circled 'em twice

Ky Ebrington, graduated from Yale in 1909, was a superb athlete. He could run 100 yards under 10 flat and was a brilliant half-back, but his game was baseball. He received offers from John McGraw and Connie Mack, but his people refused to allow him to play professionally, so he moved out to Twin Falls, Idaho, and took a job with the South Side Irrigation Company.

Twin Falls was then represented in the unclassified Southern Idaho League, which offered a Sunday afternoon game, as well as a twilight performance each Wednesday. Ky became the Ty Cobb of the league almost at once.

One Wednesday evening, Twin Falls was playing Burley at home when Ky hit a single to deep center. The Burley center-fielder was tardy retrieving the ball. Ky therefore took a wide turn at first and started for second. He arrived just as the throw-in was being received by Doc Nogley, Burley dentist and second-baseman.

Ky immediately set sail for third and Doc was so startled that he went into a psychological freeze. Ky scored, of course standing up.

The Burley manager came raging from his bench. "Doc," he yelled, "in God's name why didn't you throw that ball?"

And Doc, who was still clutching the ball with both hands, replied, "I was—I was—just waitin' for the son-of-a-bitch to come around again!"

Them odds, kid

Some years ago, when the then Brooklyn Dodgers opened the season by winning ten straight, I offered to bet my friend, the late Carl P. Zimmerer, flaming Dodger fan, a million dollars to one that his heroes would not take all of their remaining games.

The odds vastly appealed to him, then the gleam left his eyes after a moment's thought and he said, "You son-of-a-bitch, you haven't *got* a million dollars. You couldn't pay me if you lost!"

FOOTBALL

Just a little early

An institution in the Southwest had a semi-professional football team, the star of which was a halfback called "Half-Spin" Jones because of his ability to spin his way out of the encircling arms of tacklers. Jones was believed to be dissipating, but he was so outstandingly his outfit's paramount performer that neither his coach nor any of his teammates dared to upbraid him. That responsibility was, therefore, passed along to the president of the institution.

Jones appeared in prexy's office at 9:00 on a Monday morning. There was a brief exchange of amenities. Then prexy, fixing Jones with a cold, beady glance, asked harshly, "Jones, do *you* drink?" The young man licked his lips slightly and a mild gleam came into his eyes as he replied, "Well, Doc, it's kinda early in the mornin'. But never let it be said that old Jonesey ever let a pal drink alone!"

Calories did count

In the long ago, when Idaho had football teams that could compete in the Pacific Coast conference, that institution boasted a magnificent guard named

Nelson ("Nellie") Armstrong. He was big, fast, powerful; made several all-Pacific Coast teams; was chosen to play in the East-West Shrine game. But he had an insatiable appetite. He always had three or four helpings of whatever was served at the training table and still walked away unsatisfied.

Idaho was playing Oregon at home; the score was tied at 7 to 7 and Idaho had the ball on the one-yard line, fourth down and 90 seconds to play. Time was called. When play was resumed, the stands were screaming and the nerves of the other 21 boys on the field were as taut as piano strings. But Nellie was relaxed.

The Idaho quarterback went up and down the line slapping rear elevations. Coming to Nellie, he administered a sharp crack and shouted, "We're gonna drive 'er over, Nellie, old boy. How do yah feel, kid? How do yah feel?"

Nellie half-turned and replied calmly, "I feel all right, but I'm awful Goddam hungry!"

The touchdown was scored over Nellie.

First things first, professor

The football coach at one of Pennsylvania's anthracite colleges had gone down to the 5000-feet level of a local mine and discovered a magnificent prospect: six feet four inches tall, 240 pounds, the reflexes of a tiger, a potential all-American. The phenomenon was signed up for a grant-in-aid immediately, but he only had gone through the sixth grade. Therefore he had to submit to an entrance examination and the mathematics professor flunked him.

Wildly infuriated, the coach went raging to his academic colleague. "Doc, how could you do it?" he screamed. "You have denied an opportunity for higher education to this glorious specimen of young Pennsylvania manhood. You have done the gravest possible disservice to this institution and to the whole American way of life! Doc, how could you?"

"But, coach," replied the professor, "I only asked the boy what 7 and 7 were. And he said 15. I couldn't overlook that."

"Well, you shoulda overlooked it. You shoulda overlooked it. Goddlemighty, he only missed it by three."

Scholarships ain't for scholars

Pete Reich, then all-Eastern guard and football captain at Dartmouth, where there is a strong tendency to play students, had met, at Christmas time, a thick-muscled high school teammate who had gone to one of the Southeastern Conference institutions on a scholarship which had nothing to do with scholarship. After the usual small talk, Pete asked the young man what courses he was taking.

"Well, pal," came the reply, "I'm takin' physical education and I'm takin' square dancin'." Then the boy paused and an embarrassed grin spread over his lumpy features as he added, "Y'know, Pete, I just can't rightly remember the name of that third damn' course!"

[At the institution in question, football players were permitted to read newspapers in class, but they were sternly forbidden to rattle them.]

Who doesn't mix metaphors?

Professor Glen Rainey of Georgia Tech tells about a remedial course in spelling (offered at another institution) for the dull and muscular.

The thick-necked young man on his feet booted the first word given him and the instructor said, "Strike one!"

Another word; another distressing fumble; and the call, "Strike two!"

Then from the middle of the class room came an earnest exhortation, "Make him pitch to you, kid!"

This listener listened

Dan McGugin, Vanderbilt's stalwart football coach for many years, had been an immovable guard on the devastating point-a-minute teams developed at Michigan by Fielding H. ("Hurry-up") Yost. The two men married sisters and were understanding and affectionate brothers-in-law, but each of them found a practical joke hard to resist.

In the early 1930's, Hurry-up had been named principal speaker at the annual meeting of the nation's football coaches to be held in New York City. And he took his responsibility seriously. Dan met him at Chicago and they took a drawing-room for their railroad trip to the metropolis.

Hurry-up had sweated over his speech. He had carefully written it out, memorized it, and then made Dan a captive audience as he rehearsed it at least seven or eight times.

The Michigan hero was ready for the crowning post-prandial effort of his career when the great night came, but an innocent toastmaster called on Dan first. And McGugin delivered Yost's speech, to the last gesture and syllable.

Forgiveness was finally offered, but grave coolness persisted between the brothers-in-law over a period of weeks.

TRACK

This one had a long run

Lou Merwin was captain of the University of California track team of 1896, the first group of thinclads from that state to invade the East. These stalwarts were as successful as their long line of successors, strong in all the track and field events, and the possessors of other unusual qualities. Not the least was the talent of the team's sprinter, Jim Noggert, who could produce, on demand and in the number and volume desired, what the Cascaret advertisements used to refer to as "those awful noises."

After a dual meet with Yale, the Eli half-miler might say to his California rival, "I had a hard time getting my second wind this afternoon" and the Californian would immediately boast about Noggert's remarkable gifts. Skepticism was almost always expressed and a demonstration followed. Then the Yales would offer to bet that Jim could not produce 10 in succession, then 20, then 50. That California team went home with a large part of the undergraduate money on six Eastern campuses.

Ten years afterward, in Goldfield, Nevada, Lou Merwin told the Noggert story to a fellow engineer who was loudly and openly scornful. This time the wager mounted to drinks for the entire camp, with Reg Murray, who had been the weight man on Lou's California team and was then sports cartoonist on the old New York *Evening World,* as the sole and final arbiter.

Lou's telegram to Murray read:

> Controversy here concerning James Noggert's remarkable annular development.

Please wire confirmation and best record.

Murray responded promptly:

> Have forgotten whether Noggert's Philadelphia record was 300 or 500, but not even 1000 would have feazed him. It was just as easy as puffing a pipe.

Twenty additional years passed and I related the Merwin-Noggert saga to J. M. B. Hoxsey, then head of the Committee on Stock List of the New York Stock Exchange. Hoxsey loved a story even more than a bull market and his laughter was ordinarily warm and enthusiastic, but this time he contented himself with a gentle smile. "I hate to top your story, Janx," he said, "but there was a well-authenticated Johns Hopkins case celebrating a genius who could whistle with his. No operatic arias, my dear Janx, but all the simpler melodies!"

GOLF, WHY NOT?

Pastoral profanity

Mr. Justice Owen J. Roberts played golf frequently with the Rev. Dr. Ambrose Morton at Chevy Chase. They were closely matched and they ended the 1925 season in a tight contest which found them even as they approached the eighteenth green. Justice Roberts's ball was in the "frog hair," but Dr. Morton, an eager competitor, discovered his not only trapped, but also buried in a cavernous heel print.

The reverend gentleman looked down at his ball, over at Roberts, down at his ball, ground his teeth and remained intensely quiet for at least 60 seconds.

"My dear Doctor," observed Roberts, "that quite certainly was the most profane silence ever listened to by a justice of the Supreme Court."

Couldn't be my honor?

George Bendman, who played his first golf, as a caddy, in Taft's administration and who had broken 100 only twice in the years between, was performing in a fivesome at the Farmington Country Club, near Charlottesville, Virginia, last June. Of course the honor went to individuals and, for 16 weary holes, George had not achieved that distinction. When he produced a rare par, someone else either tied him or came up with a birdie. He usually was not even close.

Then at the 160-yard, downhill 17th, George sank his tee shot with a No. 4 wood. After his competitors had putted, he swaggered up to the 18th tee and inquired loudly, "Did any of you sons-of-bitches beat a one?"

THE THREE-SHELL GAME
Well, it's called a "game"

The pool and billiard parlor in Wallace, Idaho, was operated for long years by "Whisperin' Phil" Arntrop, whose many callings included the skilled operation of a three-shell game with two carnivals and a small circus which played the eastern seaboard. This is Phil's own story:

"I got my nickname in Rock Hill, South Carolina. The bearded lady dropped her whiskers. One of the boys accidentally slugged the mayor and a dust-up was on. The 'Hey, Rube' call went out, but we couldn't handle the crowd and I caught a tent stake smack in my Adam's apple. That held me down to whisperin' from then on, so shell games and barkin' was out for me. We all had our bumps and bruises, but got away alive. I jumped the show in Kingstree, South Carolina, and finally drifted out here to Wallace, where I found a friend.

"He left me his pool hall and things has been good. I taught lots of good pool players, includin' the Moe boys, and I run a decent place, even if nobody ever asked me to teach Sunday school.

"In June, 1906, I learned that Brandt's Grand Carnival with Supreme Sideshows would play Wallace and I dropped over to nearby Kellogg to catch it. Had a hard look, but didn't see anybody I knew and I was sure nobody recognized me.

"Two mornings later I was in the law office of John Gray, who had friends from Stanly Easton, top boss of the Bunker Hill and Sullivan Mines down to me and below and who would always listen. 'John,' says I without too much palaver, 'is it all right to cross a double-crosser or slicker a slicker? John smiled his broad smile and he says, 'Phil, my boy, such folk are fair game any time. The season is always open.' So I made my plans.

"When the carny appeared, I went out, with most of the money in town on my hip and began to play the shell game. It was the usual: 'Now you see it and now you don't. Where is the little pea? Th' hand is quicker than th' eye. I believe that, my friends, and that's th' way I'm willin' to bet. Step right up, gentlemen. Step up and try your luck.'

"I bet ten dollars and lost. Then a shill—I spotted him easy—put up twenty and won. I bet twenty and this time I won. So I bet ten and lost. Then five and won. By this time, the workman thought he could cash in, so he says, 'Ain't there any sportin' blood in this camp? You can see th' odds work against me. Who would like to bet some important dough?'

"I backed away and called over seven or eight of the boys. We got into a private knot and talked and talked. Anyhow for fifteen or twenty minutes.

"Then I finally walked up to the operator and I says, 'Mister, there is money in this camp and there is sportin' money. We're goin' to call your bluff. How much can you cover? We got $4000. You can have all or any part of it.'

"He talked to *his* boys and says, 'That's just fine. We got $4000 right here and we're ready to put it up. One spin of the shells! All or nothin'! Who'll be the stakeholder? I suggest that gentleman standin' over there.' And he pointed to his own shill.

" 'No,' I says, 'How about that nice, little boy. He's got an honest face. He should satisfy everybody.' And I pointed to Eddie Fainsworth, who looked about 14, but who was 26 and had been a jockey and a good one until he broke his right shoulder so bad he couldn't hold a horse.

"Eddie was given the $8000, but the shill moved

in behind him and my friend Stanley McDonegall stood right beside the shill. Stan took out his pocket knife, opened up a sharp, four-inch blade and began to pare his fingernails with it.

"Then the routine began: 'Here we are! Here we are! Watch the shells and watch my hands. We shuffle the shells and we drop the pea so fast I'd have to guess myself. There it is! Now pick it, my friend. Show me the shell with the pea under it!'

"So I move quick and pick up the second shell. And there was the pea under it! 'Hooray,' I yelled, 'We win!'

"The shill clamps his long hands around little Eddie's neck, but Stan drives three inches of blade into the fat part of the shill's rear. He throws up his hands. Eddie gets away, sprints into town and puts our money in the Wallace National Bank.

"I have known better losers in my day. They say the most *disagreeable* things! About my mother and my grandmother and all that. But it was only talk, because Sheriff Barney Oldcamp just happened to be there with two of his deputies and seven other boys he had deputized special and who had bright, shiny stars on their chests.

"The carny left town that night and Wallace had itself quite a time.

"And the pea? *Any* chowderhead should know that the pea was *my* pea!"

POKER

This is a game of skill

Nobody was shot when five aces made their appearance in the wide-open poker game played in Boise, Idaho's Overland Bar before this dismal century arrived. The deck's joker was almost invariably used and it both was another ace and could fill straights or flushes.

On this notable occasion, the contestant on the dealer's left opened a jack pot. He had customers for several rounds, but betting before the draw promptly developed into a contest between this citizen and a single aggressive opponent. Gold and currency in large amounts were on the table before cards were demanded.

The opener said, "I'll take one." He added, "I'm going to split my openers." And he turned a king face up.

At that moment, the only other man left in the game re-examined his hand with assurance and stood pat. He had a double-ace spade flush (the spade ace and the joker) and, on the natural assumption that the opener was drawing to either a straight or a flush, his confidence was serene. For his hand plainly would beat any other flush except that rare phenomenon, a straight flush.

Betting was so brisk and determined that more than $32,000 decorated the table before the double-ace-flush contestant, finally catching a faint whiff of Gorgonzola, called the last bet.

The opener laid down four queens. Uproar ensued. Strong epithets were used and mayhem was attempted. But the law-abiding prevailed and the pot was impounded in the First National Bank upon the understanding that an appeal would be taken to the Police Gazette. That oracle's reply is an Idaho classic: "Conversation wins and loses no money in a poker game and four queens beat a double-ace flush."

The winner became a pariah, but $32,000 was consequential dough in that distant era. Income taxes took no cut from any pots whatever. Mortimer Caplin had not been born.

BOXING

There was once a white hope

Joel L. Priest reported this aftermath from the then significant trouncing of Jim Jeffries by Jack Johnson in Reno, Nevada, on July 4, 1910. Poor old Jim had been persuaded to return to the ring wars as a "white hope" to regain the heavyweight championship of the world from Jack Johnson, the colored title-holder. Jack toyed with Jim and finally, mercifully, administered a thunderous knockout in the fifteenth round.

Reno of 1910 could not accommodate the demand for hotel accommodations and passengers on special trains slept in parked Pullman cars. The morning after the fight, Joel was awakened by the porter's chanting. His obviously improvised, happy tune was sung *sotto voce,* but over and over again. The words came through with edged clarity:

"Wake up, white folks, and look at the sun,
And I'll tell you what Jack Johnson done."

ACADEME, SHADES OF

Teachers, especially college teachers, who cannot smile at their errors and themselves are in a parlous state. They have to face the same groups of the intelligent and the up-coming day after day. If they bluff, they are stupid. If they don't know, they must confess that fact right now. Moreover, they must employ humor both to rivet attention and to dissipate exacerbation. Even the dullest subject can be made tolerable by occasional apposite and honest laughter. And the better the repertoire, the greater the likelihood that that solid truth may rise from mustiness and achieve acceptance.

If this section has a law school flavor, personal experience is responsible. For I wielded a hoe in that field.

Sequitur inexorable

I am informed that one or two of Harvard's less inhibited professors may still tell this story in their law classes as an example of the completely inexorable and irresistible *sequitur*. Well, it just *might* be Yale.

In all events, a substantial Vermont farm had been sold and the sole argument remaining between the parties involved a handsome and valuable manure pile. The buyer claimed, of course, that the accumulation was real property—a fixture—and therefore remained with the land, while the seller urged that it was personal property and that his right to remove it was obvious.

The discussion continued until the seller inquired, "May I ask you just two or three questions, Mister?"

"Why certainly."

"Are cows personal property?"

"No doubt about it."

"Is grass personal property?"

"Yep."

"Then you tell me: Just how in the hell can personal property eat personal property and crap real estate?"

Blue-books: their content

Percy Corbett, Oxonian and distinguished scholar, served as professor of international law at McGill, Yale, Princeton and the University of Virginia. He was a member of Yale's committee for academic advancement when he met on campus the late Whitney Griswold, afterwards president of Yale, but then a candidate for promotion to full professor. Griswold was carrying a heavy load of examination blue-books under his left arm and Corbett inquired facetiously, "Well, Whit, what have you got there?"

Griswold groaned and replied, "Ah, my dear Percy, the vomit returns to its dog!"

Corbett says that he never voted for a colleague's promotion with greater enthusiasm.

Resources impose obligations

This also is Percy Corbett's:

Arthur Smith, long ago Master of Balliol College, Oxford, was the father of thirteen living children, only one of them—the last—a boy. Prime Minister Herbert Asquith and Smith were warm friends and Asquith had arranged to come down to Oxford on an October evening in 1913 to have dinner with the family. His train from London was late, so that he arrived after the Smiths had begun their meal.

"Ah, Master," Asquith exclaimed, "I continue to marvel at your magnificent resources."

"My dear Prime Minister," Smith replied, "my problem is *husbanding* my resources."

Professor to professor

One of the great intellectual *tours de force* of this generation was an address, "Chief Justices I Have Known," delivered by Justice Felix Frankfurter before a University of Virginia audience in

June, 1953. Justice Frankfurter spoke for two hours, analyzing personalities, citing instances and episodes, quoting from decisions of the Supreme Court, all without a scrap of paper before him. His performance was stunning.

Rugged chairs for an overflow audience had been largely provided by local undertakers, so that, despite Justice Frankfurter's brilliance, caudal trauma had become endemic before his peroration was delivered. When the Justice sat down, the presiding student, E. Barrett Prettyman, Jr., of Washington, D. C., said that Justice Frankfurter had graciously consented to answer questions.

The first person to stand up was Professor Charles O. Gregory, who had known Justice Frankfurter on a first-name basis for many years and who refreshingly and invariably speaks his mind.

"I am delighted, Charlie," said the Justice. "Did you get up to ask a question?"

"Hell, no, Felix." Gregory replied. "I just got up to go home!"

Few gatherings have disintegrated more rapidly or more happily.

And what league, Dad?

Oscar, the teen-age son of a professor of English at Washington and Lee, was interested in baseball, not at all in his studies at a good preparatory school. But his father became encouraged when the young man seemed slightly enthused about a course in general European history. Probing a little, the professor asked, when Oscar next came home, "Son, who was Copernicus? Tell me something about Copernicus."

The smallest gleam shone in Oscar's eyes and he said, "I think I've got it! Can't you give me just a little hint, Dad? What position did he play?"

This one can be told in Mississippi

The Supreme Court's momentous decision of 1954 in the *Brown* case had just been announced. Professor Hardy Dalmington of the University of Alabama was introduced, at a Chicago meeting, to one Terence Aloysius O'Neil, who declared that he was a trustee of Notre Dame.

"I would like to have you know, Professor Dalmington," said O'Neil, "that we already have completely solved the problem of integration at Notre Dame. They attend our classes; they eat in our dining halls; they sleep in our dormitories; they participate fully in our college activities; they are among our most prominent athletes."

"That is extremely interesting, Mr. O'Neil. How many negroes do you have on the Notre Dame campus?"

"Negroes? Negroes? Who said anything about negroes? I have been talking about Protestants!"

Blackjack, Incorporated

I had a large class (about 200) when I began to teach corporation law at the University of Virginia Law School a dozen years ago. Proceeding alphabetically, I called, one February morning, on a lad named Pat Hale. Pat responded adequately, but I failed to make the proper notation in my rollbook and committed the heinous error of calling on him again two days later. The young man once more recited excellently, but a smile circled the room and I said, realizing what I had done, "Mr. Hale, I assure you that the next time I reach your name, I shall temper justice with mercy."

In about six weeks, the "H's" came up again and I said, "Mr. Hale, do you know anything about the game called blackjack or twenty-one?"

"Why, yes, suh, I have played the game."

"Mr. Hale, you have two eminently sound recitations to your credit. Would you like to stand on 17 or would you care to draw a card?"

And Hale replied, to the intense satisfaction of classmates and professor, "You may hit me, suh!"

Why not try?

Professor Charles O. Gregory of the University of Virginia, a recognized authority in the field of labor law, who also taught aspirants to bench and bar at Wisconsin and Chicago, was asked whether it would be feasible to unionize a law school faculty.

"Hell," he replied, "it would be easier to unionize a zoo!"

Surprise and the Dean of Women

At Ouachita College years ago, dates were permitted only on Friday and Saturday nights, but a brash young man, smitten by sweet Agnes Branson on a Tuesday afternoon, called at the girls' dormitory later that evening. Met by the Dean of Women, he demanded the privilege of a visit with Agnes.

"But my youthful friend," said the Dean, "don't you realize that you men students are permitted to see the girls only on Friday and Saturday nights? Please don't ask me to break the rules!"

"This is an emergency. This is different. And I don't even want her to know who I am. I want to surprise her. You see, I'm her brother."

"She'll be surprised, all right. But how do you think I feel? I'm her mother!"

The philosopher and the fly

One of Harvard's professors of philosophy, reading the *New York Times* in a favorite restaurant while his breakfast coffee cooled, suddenly noticed a fly in his cup. He shouted for a waiter and inquired sternly, "What's *he* doing in there?" "Hmm," replied the waiter, "Hmm! I would say that he is swimming the breast stroke."

Excavations have their uses

The University of North Carolina, at Chapel Hill, was proceeding with the construction of its new gymnasium and, in the process, a huge excavation had been dug. Dean Brandis Wettach was observing the activity when one of the town's characters approached him to ask, "Dean, how come that big hole? What they gonna do with that big hole?"

"Osbert," the dean replied sternly, "they expect to put every single son-of-a-bitch in Chapel Hill in that hole!"

"Hm-m-m! Hm-m-m! Who we gonna git to cover 'em up?"

Grades for athletes

Flagabama University, becoming more academically-minded, required holders of athletic scholarships to rank in the upper half of their courses or forfeit all special privileges. One of the less enlightened among them, although thoroughly equipped with "gut" or "crip" subjects, needed one more in order to be sure of staying eligible. Therefore he selected Basket Weaving, only to discover that the nine other students in the course were Seminole Indians and that the instructor graded on a "curve"!

Be prompt, my learned friend

As a teacher of law, I had some difficulty in persuading my students that punctuality *is* the "courtesy of kings and the duty of all gentle folk everywhere." And I presented the problem to the late Bolitha J. Laws, then Chief District Judge in the District of Columbia, asking how he handled members of the bar who were inclined to tardiness.

"I do not have the least trouble," he said. "If a lawyer has an appointment before me at 9:30 in the morning and he appears at 9:30, plus 30 seconds, I fine him $25 for contempt of court."

"But, Judge Laws," I inquired, "what about second offenders?"

"My dear Professor Gussman," he replied with a tight smile, "there *are* no second offenders!"

LAWYERS AND JUDGES

This will be a reasonably substantial section. Until my retirement, I had spent the larger part of my adult life among lawyers and judges. And examination of them from beyond the pale has not materially altered my affection and respect. This much must be said: Even a run-of-the-mill client who confronts a lawyer and declares, "Listen, you illegitimate, you're wrong!" is likely to evoke a grin rather than the offended mien of a small nature. Lawyers often are publicly, demonstrably, wrong. Juries tell them. So do judges. And even members of the judiciary may be informed that they are gapingly in error. Five (sometimes four) justices of the United States Supreme Court have the last word, but nobody is required to agree with them. Furthermore, they endure the most simmering criticism in silence.

JUDGES! BLESS THEIR FREQUENTLY KIND HEARTS!

Metamorphosis

Judge Ovard Minkroop of the United States District Court in Memphis, Tennessee, was well and unfavorably known for his physical and intellectual inertness. He took forever to decide cases;

his absences from the bench were both unaccounted for and frequent.

When it was announced one morning that another judge would take His Honor's calendar call, one of the lawyers asked what was the matter with Judge Minkroop.

"Didn't you know?" Walter Ganstrong replied, "The judge has a bad attack of swodoposis."

"In Heaven's name, what is swodoposis?"

"My good friend, swodoposis is that peculiarly and poignantly painful ailment in which the iron in the blood has been metamorphosed into lead in the ass!"

Gamblers in the courtroom

Judge Cassidy, who presided over a Butte, Montana, court of original, unlimited jurisdiction in another era, had a unique personal eccentricity. He pulled hairs from his nose as he ruled on the evidence in a closely contested case.

One afternoon, two of Butte's then numerous gamblers were in the courtroom. With nothing better to occupy his time, Flannery bet Moskop, after some negotiations, that the judge would extract five hairs in ten minutes.

Almost at once, His Honor said, "Objection sustained!" and yanked a hair. "Overruled!" and another hair gone. "Sustained!" accompanied by the removal of a third filament.

Then the judge's right hand wandered down toward the seat of his chair and Flannery exclaimed, "All bets is off! The old son-of-a-bitch is dealin' from the bottom of the deck!"

Glamour and the public payroll

Chief Judge Simon E. Sobeloff of the United States Court of Appeals for the Fourth Circuit says that his distinguished senior colleague, Judge Morris A. Soper, presiding in Baltimore's municipal court many years ago, had under consideration a petition for increased alimony. The defendant was a street-cleaner who urged that his former wife's demands exceeded his total compensation.

"But Your Honor," the lady contended, "he keeps his lousy job as a street-cleaner just so I can't live the way I should. Why, if he only got into business, what you call this here free enterprise, he could easy make enough to support me right. And I want you to make him do it."

Judge Soper smiled, looked out of the window, and replied gently, "But, madam, do you give no consideration whatever to the glamour of public office?"

Not in this courtroom, counselor

Federal District Judge Manton Mintone of Arkansas was allergic to distracting noises in his courtroom. Gus Lasley of Little Rock knew of his Honor's quiddity, but he had been absent-mindedly jingling silver coins in a trousers pocket. His boiling point reached, the judge spoke sharply, "Mr. Lasley, how much money do you have in that pocket?"

Gus counted and replied, "Exactly $2.90, Your Honor."

"Well, you are hereby fined $2.80 for contempt of court. Pay the clerk and then see if you can rattle that damn' dime!"

That's what the judge told him

When an unsophisticated witness addressed himself exclusively to the judge in a Richmond, Virginia, courtroom not long ago, His Honor admonished, "Speak to the jury, Mr. Witness. Speak to the jury!"

The witness turned to the jury box. "Hello!" he said.

Those questions from their Lordships

Oral argument ordinarily is not restricted before Canadian tribunals and the Chief Commissioner of that surging nation's Board of Transport Commissioners apologized because the argument in an important freight-rates proceeding would be limited to seven days.

He said that the members of the Board would restrain *themselves* and told about a young barrister named Bryson-Smyth who was presenting his first argument before Great Britain's Privy Council. He had been harassed and confused by their Lordships' numerous questions until the mighty Lord Carson leaned across the bench and asked, "Mr. Bryson-Smyth, isn't this the major point you are presenting to us?" Then Carson proceeded to state the youthful barrister's position with characteristic lucidity and the young man replied, "I am deeply grateful, m'Lord! Your Lordship has put my proposition infinitely better than I could." Carson answered, "Ah yes, Mr. Bryson-Smyth, but you see I had the supreme advantage of not being interrupted!"

Who's asking the questions?

Arthur Brown, who practiced in Salt Lake City, Utah, at the turn of the century, carried on a bitter personal vendetta with the local United States District Judge, Oscar Botney.

Judge Botney was given to asking questions from the bench and in a case which found Brown representing the plaintiff, His Honor put one of his usual inquiries to a witness.

"If the Court please," said Brown, "if you are asking that question on behalf of the defendant, I object to it as grossly and obscenely irrelevant and immaterial. If you are asking it on behalf of the plaintiff, I withdraw it!"

Courtesy to a judge on the witness stand

On another occasion, Judge Botney appeared as a witness in one of the state courts. When he responded, "I don't know," to a question from his own counsel, Brown leaped to his feet. "I object to this witness going into what he does not know," he thundered. "That, I submit, will open entirely too wide a field!"

Justices Story and Douglas

At a New York City banquet held in 1939, the extraordinary Owen D. Young was introducing Justice William O. Douglas, who had then just been named to the United States Supreme Court and who was the youngest person ever appointed to that tribunal, except for the legendary Justice Story.

Mr. Young said that it had been the duty of the youthful Justice Story to observe the weather just before the noon conference of the justices and that if he could announce a dismal prospect, superior Kentucky bourbon was served to the members of the Court. One day, however, Story could see only brilliant sunshine flooding the entire District of Columbia and he rose to declare, "Mr. Chief Justice Marshall, the jurisdiction of this Court is unusually broad and surely, surely somewhere in this vast domain, it must be dark and dreary!"

Then Mr. Young turned to the honored guest. "Mr. Justice Douglas," he said, "I do not know whether you, as the youngest justice, are still required to perform that important function. But precedents are strong in the Supreme Court of the United States. Or at least they used to be!"

Advocacy from the bench

In a Virginia courtroom, responsibility for examining all witnesses had been assumed by His Honor.

Peter Inmont, counsel for the plaintiff, was pleased by both questions and responses and had become agreeably relaxed when the judge's interrogation took a different and potentially unfortunate direction. Turning on a high-candle power smile, Inmont got to his feet: "If the Court please, I do not object in the least to having Your Honor take over this case, but for God's sake, *don't lose it!*"

Tyrants and tobacco juice

United States District Judge Mingtley, who presided in a Southern city, was one of the more exacerbating judicial tyrants of his era. He was sarcastic, irritable, sadistic, discourteous, the terror of witnesses and counsel alike.

This particular morning, he had mercilessly ridden Fred Ortborn, a highly respected leader of the local bar, sneering, snarling, needling and making himself as disagreeable as possible. Among the judge's less couth habits was tobacco chewing. Two cuspidors were placed near his bench, but he missed both of them more often than not and, in the process, copiously freckled his judicial gown with dark dribblings.

When a recess was called, Ortborn asked if he might approach the bench. Grudging permission was granted and Fred came forward.

"Your Honor," he said eye-to-eye, "I deem it my bounden duty to report that *some* son-of-a-bitch is spitting all over this Court!"

Why should a motorist win?

When the judge of a lower Virginia court, deciding his first case, found a motorist guilty of the high crime of following an ambulance too closely, an appeal was taken. The appellate tribunal was unable to discover statutory justification for sustaining the verdict. But reversal would have done violence to the judicial bond in such circumstances. The defendant was, therefore, convicted for unauthorized practice of the law.

Don't touch my sentence, Mr. Registrar

The late Lord Barksdale, judge of the King's Bench, believed that the lifting of one's voice above an ordinary conversational tone was beneath the dignity of a British jurist.

In George V's reign, his Lordship was presiding at the trial of a Sussex defendant for what had been a peculiarly aggravated and unjustified assault with a deadly weapon. Community indignation was at a high pitch. The jury said "Guilty" almost immediately and Lord Barksdale, speaking in his modulated conversational style, said, "I sentence you to a term of four years at penal servitude."

The defendant's face remained blank and continued to be expressionless when his Lordship repeated the sentence. This brought the Registrar to his feet to observe that the defendant was deaf, that he could not hear what had been told him.

"Mr. Registrar," instructed Lord Barksdale calmly, "Repeat the sentence."

Again the Registrar gained his feet. "Listen, you son-of-a-bitch," he shouted, "The Judge says you're going to jail for five years! How do you like that?"

"Mr. Registrar," his Lordship observed, "I do not object to your characterization of the defendant. Indeed, it seems to me in the circumstances not without its measure of appropriateness. But I must object to your increasing my sentence!"

Ah, but it isn't

Abraham Wilson of New York reports that a British judge, sitting in the Isle of Wight, was about to pass sentence on a convicted bigamist. His Lordship, a bachelor, observed sententiously, "Bigamy is having one wife too many." Then he paused and added, "So also is monogamy."

LAWYERS: IN THE COURTROOM AND OUT

Not my mitt, pal

Judge Samuel S. Leibowitz has related that, within a few months after entering the practice, he was visited (in an office he then shared with a "realtor") by a tall and cadaverous citizen who introduced himself as "Lanky the Dip."

Lanky came to his point at once. "Counselor," he said, "I've been watchin' you in court these four, five weeks and you are doin' so good I want you for my mouthpiece. They got me up for pickin' a guy's pocket, but it's a bum rap. I'm tellin' you, counselor, I didn't do it. This lug says he felt my mitt in his pocket, but he's a cheap stoolie. I been pickin' pockets for 15 years and I'm a top worker. *Nobody* never felt *my* mitt in his pocket."

Leibowitz accepted the assignment and carefully placed in his pocketbook the $100 bill given him by way of retainer. Lanky went his way and the young lawyer cried jubilantly, "Nellie, we're in business! Come here and let me show you!" Then he began to look for his money, slapping his pockets, opening desk drawers and finally becoming a little frantic. It was not to be found.

After 15 agonizing minutes, Lanky reappeared and delivered the pocketbook. "Counselor," he said, "I just wanted to give you that old confeedence! Nobody, but nobody, never felt *my* mitt in his pocket!"

Persona non grata

Richmond, Virginia, had a streetcar strike long years ago. The adversaries were far apart. Feeling ran high. But there had been no rioting until counsel for the company (I shall misname him George Brantling) appeared at a meeting of the strikers. George was the Beau Brummel of Richmond's bar—razor-edge trousers, a waxed moustache, pink-striped shirts, personal elegance; furthermore, he believed that his was the *first,* first family of Virginia.

Fists flew and two of the strikers were arrested for assault. George was an important witness when the case came on for trial and he was cross-examined by a thoroughly country-boy lawyer representing the strikers. After leading George through parts of his direct evidence, the country lawyer said, "Mr. Brantling, didn't you come to the meeting for the special purpose of provokin' my clients?"

"No, I can't say that I did."

"But you must have known that there would be some kind of a dust-up when you stuck your head in that room. Ain't that so?"

"Well, suh, I realized that I was *persona non grata.*"

The countryman stopped short.

In his argument two days later he said, "Gentlemen of the Jury, I suppose that y'all noticed that I quit cold, cross-examinin' Mr. Brantlin', when he said he realized that he was *persona non grata.* My dear friends, I *had* to quit. I just didn't know what that Eyetalian stuff meant. But I found out. I was talkin' to one of my Eytalian friends last night and I asks him, 'What was that George Brantlin' spoutin' when he said he realized that he was *persona non grata?*' My friend he says, 'Brantlin' meant he realized he was a stuffy old bastard.' And, gentlemen of the jury, he *was!* That's what caused all the trouble."

Brantling had to be physically restrained by a bailiff. The defendants were promptly acquitted.

Persuasion at a high point

Bob Henderson was representing one of the Florida utilities before a trial examiner of the Securities and Exchange Commission in the later 1930's. This was at a time when trial examiners did not even squirm under the pressed-down thumbs of commission counsel and when they passed off even the most strenuous objections to evidence with a casual, "Aw, I'll let it in for what it's worth."

One of the more odious documents of that era was the so-called "Murphy letter," an outrageous piece of hanky-panky which gave ugly expression to concepts of the bad, old days and which then counsel for the Securities and Exchange Commission and the Federal Power Commission put into all their records, plainly for the purpose of smearing Murphy and those who had been his associates.

The Murphy letter had as little relevance as a Southern Pacific time table for 1877 in the proceeding Bob had in hand, but Commission counsel marked it for identification and Bob knew that the complaisant examiner would admit it if it were presented.

"Are you going to offer the Murphy letter?" Bob asked.

"Of course I am!"

"No you're not."

"Who says so?"

"I say so. If you offer it, I'm going to take you right out in the hall and get good and damn' physical with you!"

The letter did not go in.

Those bothersome beneficiaries

In the early 1930's, a Toronto lawyer friend was walking along London's Fleet Street on a warm

August afternoon when an anguished voice reached him from the open transom above the door of a solicitor's office, "But we cawn't do that! We cawn't do that! If we do that, the final controversy will be settled and the entire estate will be frittered away to the beneficiaries!"

Petrovus the litigious

One of Toronto's leading lawyers—I shall call him Cyril Tallman—somehow acquired a genuinely litigious client, Petrovus Z. Aikman, who demanded that a suit be brought, against Tallman's advice, in a Toronto District Court. He lost, insisted on an appeal to the Supreme Court of the Province of Ontario, lost again, forced Tallman to go to the Supreme Court of Canada, was trounced once more and clamored—although Tallman pleaded with him to go no further—for a final appeal (no longer available) to the Privy Council of the House of Lords.

Defeated for the last time, Aikman came to Tallman literally wringing his hands. "Mr. Tallman," he asked, "for God's sake what do I do now?"

"Go home and breed," Tallman replied. "We need your kind!"

In the guy's handwriting

George Gilbert of Charlottesville, Virginia, had brought suit, as a young lawyer, for a client who claimed that one Frederick Hendrix owed him $350 which was not paid when four heifers had been delivered. The plaintiff's case was presented and then, to Gilbert's utter discomfiture, Hendrix took the stand and offered receipts, in the plaintiff's handwriting, evidencing payment of the entire indebtedness.

The plaintiff leaped up and shook his fist at Hendrix. "Why you lousy bastard," he shouted, "if you hadn't told me you had lost them receipts, I wouldn't never sued ya'!"

Informing the senior partner's wife

Tom Mahony of Boston, widely known international lawyer, former president of the Catholic International League for Peace, had gone to his office one morning when his delightful wife, Mary, discovered a large hole in the middle of Beacon Street, just in front of their home. Mary called the office, but Tom was in court and other partners were not available. Mary said that she had to talk with a lawyer and was connected with a young man named Macken, who had been on the job only three months. She identified herself, told about the hole and inquired anxiously, "What shall I do?" Macken replied calmly, "Go right out and fall into it, Mrs. Mahony. The city is liable!"

Lawyers must account for their time

Graham Sumner, a Simpson Thacher & Bartlett veteran, once told me about a traditional New York lawyer who sent this bill to one of his cherished clients:

New York, N. Y.
April 2, 1904

Abner P. Morgan
to
Sullivan and Echols

Dr.

To crossing the street to confer with you and to re-crossing the street upon discovering that it was not you $50.00

Before lawyers became specialists

Arthur Brown of Salt Lake City was on his way home at six o'clock one evening when he met an acquaintance who asked a question he could not answer. Brown glared, spun on his heel and returned to his office.

Shortly after midnight, he was seen in a local bar, comfortably in the embrace of bourbon, and yet still articulate.

"Just after I left m' office tonight," he announced, "a son-of-a-bitch put one to me I couldn't handle. But I can answer the son-of-a-bitch now! I can answer him now!"

Specialization for lawyers was then some years in the future.

Surprise!

Judge Skelly Wright tells about the lawyer who asked for a further postponement as a long-deferred trial was about to begin. He said that he had been painfully surprised and therefore obviously needed time for additional preparation.

"But how can you say you are surprised?" inquired His Honor. "This case has been on the trial calendar for months. You must be ready to proceed."

"No, sir! That ain't so. Two damn' witnesses who promised me they wouldn't show up are right here in the courtroom! *I'm surprised!*"

The learned gentleman got an answer

What may be the most devastating rejoinder ever heard in an American courtroom was the end-product of a time when the far West was less inhibited than it has since become.

Elmer Arkford had arrived, fresh from law school, in a community which I shall mis-identify as Calampa. He was a virile youth and, in accordance with then custom—the year was 1884—he made what seemed appropriate arrangements with an acquiescent young woman. The alliance was terminated after several years. Elmer married a belle of the town, raised a family, and became a church vestryman.

Charles E. Maintrink, another recent law school graduate, followed Arkford to Calampa by only a few months. He also worked out an extra-marital liaison, but ultimately, after long-continued badgering and harassment, he transformed the lady into "an honest woman."

The new century was still a novelty when Arkford and Maintrink became opponents in bitter water-rights litigation. Tempers ran high and when Arkford urged the application of equitable principles, of obvious morality, Maintrink descended to the personal.

"If your Honor please," he said, "I am astonished that Mr. Arkford has the effrontery to invoke the name of equity. How can he dare to pose as a champion of morality? Why almost the whole town knows that when he first came to Calampa, he lived openly and notoriously—for three years—with a whore!"

There was a shocked silence. Arkford's balding skull turned crimson. But he did not leave his chair; nor did he raise his voice as he replied, "What Mr. Maintrink has just said is quite true. In my wild-oats days in Calampa, I did live for some years with a whore. So also did Mr. Maintrink. But there *is* a difference between us. He married his!"

A criminal lawyer reacts

This is Judge John D. Butzner's story:

Thirty years ago or more, the leading member of Norfolk's criminal bar was a vigorous practitioner disguised for these purposes as Bill Boggs. And a leader of the business community was James Henry Cabell-Cabell, president of the Norfolk Tenth National Bank, a stuffy and portentous citizen for whom Boggs had only the most dilute enthusiasm.

One Sunday afternoon in late August, Bill was luxuriating on his side porch when a policeman putted up on his motorcycle and declared, "Mr. Boggs, I have been asked to deliver the message that Mr. James Henry Cabell-Cabell wishes to see you immediately."

"Well, you go back and tell that sour slob that

I have office hours. If he wants to interview me, I'll be available in my office tomorrow morning."

"But Mr. Boggs, you don't understand. Mr. Cabell-Cabell is in jail. He wants to see you in his cell!"

Bill leaped to his feet and clapped palm to brow.

"My God!" he exclaimed, "What have they done? What have they done to that poor, innocent man?"

Argument written and read

Calampa, Oregon, had become the scene of a strongly-resisted divorce action. The parties were New Yorkers of wealth and position. Calampa counsel, including Elmer Arkford, were necessarily involved, but lawyers from both New York City and Portland, Oregon, also were brought into the case.

Early in the proceedings, Andrew Montagule, from one of the larger Portland firms, read to the court a scholarly, precise dissertation on the law of domestic relations. He stumbled, spluttered and choked over phrasing and ideas which plainly were not even casual acquaintances. Andy was a pleasant person—his firm's business-getter—but not a deep-sea lawyer.

When he sat down, Elmer Arkford asked immediately, "Andy, did you write that argument?"

"Yes, of course I wrote it! Of course I wrote it! Don't you believe me?"

"Sure, my friend. I wouldn't question your word. I do believe you. And I also would believe you if you told me that you wrote the Bible!"

Portentousness judicially confirmed

Throckmorton Jackson Leehigh was general counsel for the Keswick and Roanoke railroad. His stuffiness probably never had been surpassed at the Virginia bar. Not the most ingratiating of his habits was that of whispering vapid and persistent suggestions into the ears of local counsel who defended the Keswick in damage suits.

Old Throck was at his worst one morning when the plaintiff's lawyer characterized him after a fashion thought unkind even in the courtrooms of that day.

Local counsel for the railroad stood up and almost shouted, "If the court please, my learned friend has just referred to the Hon. Throckmorton Jackson Leehigh as a stuffy and portentous old son-of-a-bitch!"

The judge, presiding in a western Virginia county, covered a broad smile with his hand and asked, "Well, ain't he?"

Atlanta Yankee in southern Georgia

E. Smythe Gambrell of Atlanta, former president of the American Bar Association, has his less humble moments. Some time ago, he was trying a major divorce case in southern Georgia and opposition counsel consistently referred to him as a Yankee from Atlanta.

"Why, I'm no Yankee," he replied, "I was brought up in South Carolina. As a boy I plowed a mule."

"Mr. Gambrell is a lawyer of great distinction," the local lawyer rejoined, "and I suppose we have to believe him, but I ain't nevah befo' in mah whole life heard of a plow-boy named Smythe!"

Lawyers are always under oath

T. Munford Boyd of the Virginia bar was appearing, of course in association with local counsel, before a Lancaster, Pennsylvania, Commissioner authorized to deal with domestic matters. When a recess came, the Commissioner stepped down from his bench and approached the table reserved for counsel. "Mr. Boyd," he said, "I suppose that you, comin' from Virginia, are a Democrat."

Munford knew that he was deep in rock-bound Republican territory, but he believes that a gentleman is always under oath, so he replied, "Yes, Mr. Commissioner, I am a life-long Jefferson Democrat."

"Well, I want you to know," came the rejoinder, "that except for you and me, every other son-of-a-bitch in this room is a damn' Republican."

Should he have asked?

As a young lawyer, T. Munford Boyd was appointed to defend an unfortunate Virginian charged with the theft of chickens. Seeking the assurance sometimes needed in such circumstances, Boyd asked his client, "Henry, did you steal those chickens?"

There were thirty seconds of hesitation; then: "Y' know, Mistah Munny, that's the one big weakness in mah case!"

This is George Allen's story

Civil damages were being sought for attempted rape and the testimony of plaintiff and defendant was beyond reconciling. In such circumstances, the Virginia practice permits the introduction of opinion testimony as to the witness's reputation for truth-telling. And the youthful Harvard law school graduate acting for the plaintiff put on the stand a venerable, unlettered patriach.

"Mr. Manningson, do you know the plaintiff, Santhy Byrdwood?"

"Yes, suh, sho'ly do."

"How long have you known her?"

"Since she was knee-high to a duck."

"Do you know her reputation for truth and veracity in this community?"

"Yes, suh, 'spect I do."

"Well, then, you tell this court and this jury exactly what her reputation in this town for truth *and* veracity is."

"They ain't no question about her tellin' the truth. She tells the truth all right. And as fer vee-racity, some say she do and some say she don't!"

Nomenclatural hyphenation

When my partner, Bob Henderson, was in Arizona some years ago, he heard and observed the introduction of a starchy New York lawyer to a hard-bitten local rancher.

The Arizonan was slightly deaf and he asked, "What was that name again, please. I didn't quite catch it."

"My name is James Cadwadlington Cadwadlington."

"For God's sweet sake, what was that?"

"Sir, I would have you know that my name is James Cadwadlington Cadwadlington."

"H-m-m-m! James Cadwadlington Cadwadlington! Well, I'll be a son of a bitch-bitch!"

The importunate blue pencil

I was discussing with my long-time partner, Sid Barber, the draft of a brief he had prepared and, as is the way of former city-editors, I was using my pencil freely. Sid had endured my emendations for almost an hour before he inquired, "Janx, do you have a copy of the King James Version at home?"

"Why, certainly, Sid," I replied. "Why do you ask?"

"By God, I want to look at it. I'd like to see how far you have read!"

But Moses had a ghost-writer

Edwin S. Mack, of a widely-known Milwaukee firm, found it difficult to refrain from writing his own quiddities into documents prepared by his associates.

On a January morning at least 30 years ago, one of his younger partners, Peter Murphy, brought to Mr. Mack a set of corporate papers over which he had sweated agonizingly. Pete fully expected that the immediate reaction would be, "File 'em, my boy," but Mack reached for the papers with his left hand and for a pencil with his right.

Two hours later, Murphy marched back to his own office muttering hotly, "The old son-of-a-bitch, the old son-of-a-bitch".

Fred Sammond, another senior partner, heard the objurgations and asked, "What's gnawing on you, Pete?"

"I said the old son-of-a-bitch and I meant the old son-of-a-bitch! Why if that old son-of-a-bitch had been there when Moses brought the tablets of stone down from Mt. Sinai, he'd have run for a chisel!"

All qualifications, including the olfactory

Theophilus Frankling of the Twin Falls, Idaho, bar occasionally had recourse to the hair of a dog which had been his gay companion the night before. In this instance, he was trying a case before Judge Cavatrick, whose opinion of Bacchus and his sycophants was strongly negative. His Honor called Theo to the bench for a sharp rebuke, but he did not have the last word. Frankling replied, "If Your Honor's sense of justice is half as keen as your sense of smell. I have no scintilla of fear for my client."

He could pick 'em

Chauncey Blake of Madison, Wisconsin, applied a unique criterion to determine whether he wished to be associated with a particular member of the bar. He expressed the acme of his enthusiasm by saying, "That Jim Boone *smells* like a lawyer!"

When the soft answer is honest . . .

There is only one episode from my salad years as a practitioner in which I still find satisfaction.

My opponent in a case before the Idaho Public Utilities Commission was Abner Smithwright, a veteran Boise lawyer who felt that his large apartment house had been wrongly classified by the Idaho Power Company. Abner was a mighty malapropist. He once said, in presenting a purse of gold to Bishop Glorieux of the missionary district of Idaho, "Everybody coughed up for this purse, Bishop. Everybody! We're givin' it to you because you've always been a good man. You've been a good man ever since you was a little eunuch!"

In this instance, Abner said to the Commission, "I know what I am. I know what rate I ought to get. Is this young lawyer for the Power Company gonna call me some kind of a damn' hipponomous?"

My response had the virtue of being truthful: "I would not think of calling Mr. Smithwright a hipponomous or of applying to him any other unkind or opprobrious epithet. His son, Jim, who was killed in action, was my cherished friend. I have frequently been a guest in the Smithwright home, as Jim was in ours. My feeling for Mr. Smithwright is compounded of admiration, respect and affection."

Abner was so moved that he had nothing more to say. And the Commission decided against him. But that was *not* the idea.

CROSS-EXAMINATION

But be sure what the witness will say

George Bell, a hydraulic engineer who was both a genuine expert in his field and an adroit, experienced witness, was on the stand for cross-examination in an Idaho courtroom. He said "Yes" or "No" and then explained his answers fully and with devastating effect.

Opposing counsel became increasingly annoyed

and finally exclaimed, "Mr. Bell, I would like to get just one, plain unequivocal answer out of you. I would like to see if you can answer a single question without making a speech. You tell this court and this jury what two times two are!"

George removed his slide rule from its case, fiddled with it briefly and replied, "Let's see. Two times two. Three point nine eight. Three point nine nine. Call it four!"

The lawyer's case disappeared on a wave of laughter.

Sometimes they are coached

George Gilmer of Charlottesville, Virginia, reports on a Roanoke case in which he was required to rely heavily on the testimony of a witness he had not interviewed. The trial was set for 10:00 A.M., but his witness, a truck driver, did not arrive until 9:00 that same morning. Of course Gilmer was seen in close conversation with the truck driver and opposing counsel thought he could prove malign coaching. This colloquy took place on cross-examination:

"How long have you been in Roanoke, Mr. Bender?"

"I got here a little before 9:00 this morning."

"And what did you do between the time of your arrival and the opening of this case?"

"I spent every minute talking with Mr. Gilmer."
"What did you talk about?"
"About the case."
"Didn't talk about anything else?"
"No, sir, there wasn't no time to talk about anything else."
"I suppose Mr. Gilmer told you what to say when you got on the witness stand."
"Yes, sir, he certainly did."
"He did, eh! Well, you tell this Court and this jury just exactly what Mr. Gilmer told you to say!"
"He told me to tell the truth and nothing but the truth, because you was a damn' smart lawyer and you'd get me all mixed up if I didn't!"

The well-skewered lawyer

One of Cleveland's less enlightened lawyers had taken over the cross-examination of the first violinist of that community's Symphony Orchestra in a personal injury action:
"Well, Mr. Witness, so you're a fiddler."
"No, sir, I am a violinist."
"I say you're a fiddler."
"No, I repeat that I am a violinist."
"Come, come, Mr. Witness, you tell this jury the difference between a violinist and a fiddler."
"I would say precisely the same as the difference between a lawyer and a pettifogger!"

From the witness, wit hurts

Howard Toole of Missoula, Montana, was cross-examining a Butte Irishwoman strongly suspected of arson. Flames had spread from a fireplace under suspicious circumstances and Howard was trying to determine the quality of the building materials with which court and jury were concerned.

"Well, Mrs. O'Flaherty, was the fireplace two bricks thick?"

No answer.

"Was it three bricks thick? Or was it only one brick thick?"

Still no answer.

"Come, come, Mrs. O'Flaherty, how thick was the fireplace anyhow?"

"On me oath, young man, I say it was about as thick as your head!"

Butte juries have strong sympathies in those circumstances.

Don't kick 'em!

I was cross-examining the city attorney for one of the larger Texas cities. He had presented himself as an expert in the field of public utility law. But he wasn't. And I had him down and was kicking him.

My partner, Bob Henderson, came into the courtroom, watched my performance for a few minutes, walked over and hissed sharply in my ear, "Listen to me, Janx! You've got your egg. Do you want an omelet?"

I stopped then and there. But I should have put on my brakes at least ten minutes earlier.

Exasperation is not for lawyers

Former Governor John S. Battle of Virginia tells of a come-uppance administered early in the century to Judge Robert Lee Drake, long-time commonwealth's attorney (prosecuting attorney) for Albemarle County. Drake never permitted a jury to forget that his father had served on Stonewall Jackson's staff; he waved the Stars and Bars whether the occasion did or did not permit.

In this instance, Judge Drake was seeking a conviction for murder and much depended on when the asserted murder weapon had been fired. Abner Wilson, a venerable justice of the peace, testified flatly that he had examined the weapon within 24 hours after the deceased had been shot down and that it had not been fired for three days. Judge Drake, wholly unable to shake the witness on cross-examination, finally asked out of sheer exasperation, "Old man, just what do you know about firearms anyhow?"

"Judge Drake," came the firm reply, "from '61 to '65, firearms was my principal occupation."

The jury did not even leave the box.

That climactic question

Judge Lyttleton Waddell tells about a prosecution for drunken driving in which the defendant escaped injury when his automobile hurtled off the road and turned over in a deep ditch. One of Virginia's state troopers, who had arrived at the scene almost immediately, testified that the defendant had fallen heavily as he climbed up the bank to be interrogated. Then came cross-examination:

"Trooper Manning, you said the defendant fell as he struggled back up to the road. Is that correct?"

"Yes, sir."

"That bank was covered with honeysuckle, was it not?"

"Yes, sir."

"Anybody climbing that bank might have fallen after catching his foot in a loop of honeysuckle. Isn't that right?"

"Yes, sir."

"Well, you tell the Judge if there was anything, anything at all, unusual about the defendant's fall in those circumstances."

"There was one thing, sir. When the defendant

fell, he didn't even put out his arms to save himself. He fell flat on his face like the dead drunk he was!"

The witness and the land he farmed

Chief Justice Emery T. Knudson of the Idaho Supreme Court once tried a case which involved land ownership and, in particular, a sharply disputed boundary line fence. An older witness, Ralph Bland, who testified that he had been farming beyond the boundary fence for 75 years, was taken over for cross-examination:

"Mr. Bland, you say you have been farming beyond that boundary fence for 75 years. No question about that is there?"

"No, sir. There ain't."

"How old are you, Mr. Bland?"

"I'm 75 years old."

"Well, that's very interesting, Mr. Bland. I wish you would tell us the exact nature of your farming activities for the first two years of that time."

"Milkin', by God!"

No more cross-examination.

And just one "on direct"

James H. Hawley, a former Governor of Idaho, who had been William E. Borah's associate in the prosecution of Heywood, Moyer and Pettibone, was one of those rare individuals who are utterly outspoken. In his last year as a practitioner in Boise, he was outrageously leading one of his own witnesses before District Judge Brink. There were heated objections from across the table and Judge Brink finally leaned over the bench to say, "Governor Hawley, you are entirely too experienced a practitioner to persist in leading this witness. Why are you doing it?"

This was Hawley's exact reply:

"Hell, Your Honor, I wouldn't lead the son-of-a-bitch if he'd only testify the way I want him to!"

Lawyers lead with the left

My long-time partner, the late Bob Henderson, was one of only two persons I have known who had almost no sense of physical fear.

Pete Jonglinson, vice-president of a principal client, had been heavyweight boxing champion of the Pacific Coast Conference and, in his early 40's, could still move around. Pete was a delightful person when he was sober, but was difficult with two or three drinks under his hide and, at 240 pounds of solid meat, he could be a menace.

Pete and his wife and Bob and his lady were having dinner one evening at Bob's home when Pete became martini-nasty and began to abuse Mrs. Pete. Bob intervened and, with the two men on their feet, Pete said, "So you want some of it, do you!" and swung a round-house right at Bob's head.

I asked Bob, who never weighed more than 160, what he did. "Well, Janx", he replied, "I stepped inside the big stiff's swing and let him have the best left-hook I ever threw in my life."

"What happened?"

"I caught him flush on the jaw and he went down and out."

"Then what did you do?"

"I grabbed the girls and we got out of there."

"What about the next day?"

"Pete was entirely himself. He didn't even mention the episode. But he knew somebody had hit him. And he must have been pretty sure that it wasn't one of the girls!"

Answers must be responsive

Forty years ago, in the era of the complicated hypothetical question, Judge John F. MacLane began his cross-examination of Bill Gorton, chief engineer of the Idaho Public Utilities Commission, with a long hypothetical.

He cleared his throat portentously and inquired, "Now, Mr. Gorton, may I ask you what your opinion would be on the following state of facts?" Then he read four and a half closely-typed pages of detailed factual assumptions.

Gorton smiled, inclined his head, and replied, "Why of course you may ask me, Judge. Go right ahead!"

ACCOUNTING—BUT BRIEFLY

In my youth, too many accountants tended to be no more than bookkeepers. The balance sheet had to balance and $5.64 seemed just as important as $1,486,792.01, but that era has long gone. Under the influence of such leaders as George O. May, Percival Brundage, Paul Grady, Weldon Powell and others, the boys have become business statesmen, quite as able to put first things first as any of their contemporaries. Stories about their profession seem, however, to be old and weary. That hoary yarn about the veteran's secret: "The debit side is the side toward the window" is told at every other accountants' banquet. Here are three others which deserve to be heard.

They knew their percentages

Some while back, a young Electric Bond and Share Company lawyer had written a letter to one of the client companies in the system in which he used "debit" when he should have said "credit." Fortunately, Ben Brewster, then Comptroller of Bond and Share, caught the mistake and a correction was made before the letter was mailed. Of course the lawyer expressed profound gratitude to Ben, saying, "I was just 100% wrong, wasn't I?"

"Hell," Ben replied, "You were 200% wrong!"

Must a balance sheet balance?

Ben Brewster was taking a CPA examination some years earlier, along with an acquaintance who was undergoing that ordeal for the twelfth time. When a recess was called, the aspirant turned to Ben and inquired, "Brewster, what was that balance sheet answer?"

"It was precisely $1,684,413.97," said Ben.

"Yeah, I know," was the rejoinder, "but in God's dear name, Brewster, which side; which side?"

Fiction at its most vivid

The late and magnificently unorthodox Gene Fowler had done a special assignment in Alaska for the *Denver Post*. Substantial necessary expenditures had been incurred for antifreeze and drawing to inside straights. Imagination of the highest order therefore became necessary as Gene was preparing his expense account for Colonel Bonfils.

Then Gene recalled that he had been required to hire a costly dog team to perform a vital task and that the lead dog, Balno, a superb male animal, had perished in his service. Of course the owner had to be compensated generously. But not yet quite whole, Gene brought his account to a tender climax with this entry: "Flowers for bereaved bitch . . . $50.00."

RELIGION AND HUMOR

Religion and humor plainly are not consonant. One deals with ultimates: the whole reach of the supernatural, man's strange place at the "center" of an expanding universe. The other plainly is secondary, even though it ranks high among humanity's great gifts, releases tension, makes endurable even a long day on Wall Street.

There is little humor—intentional humor at least—in the Bible. Jesus must have smiled, however, when He spoke of rich men entering the Kingdom of Heaven no more easily than camels might slip through the eye of a needle, of the "mote that is in thy brother's eye" and "the beam in thine own eye" and of straining at gnats and swallowing camels.

Alfred North Whitehead has said, "The total absence of humor from the Bible is one of the most singular things in literature" and "the absence of laughter from the Hebraic religions is a serious matter to us of the Northern European races, for laughter plays a large part in our lives, and we are forced to do our laughing almost entirely outside of our religion." [1]

In all events, Jonah resisting the "great fish's" metabolic processes (Walter Roy Jones says that the Book of Jonah is a brilliant satire), and Joshua

---

[1]. *Dialogues of Alfred North Whitehead*, Price, Little, Brown; Boston, 1954, pp. 199, 456.

interrupting the inexorable movement of sun and moon for the purpose of carving up additional enemies, tickle many ribs, but not Billy Graham's.

It is natural for ministers to take themselves and their sermons seriously. They are abetted by dull parishioners. Many of them find it quite impossible to laugh at themselves. The light touch annoys them.

There have been delightful exceptions: Bishop Irving Johnson and Dean Paul Roberts of the Episcopal church; Dr. A. Powell Davies, Dr. Lon Ray Call, Dr. Jacob Trapp and the Rev. Walter Roy Jones of the Unitarian-Universalist church; Fr. Edward Conway, S.J.; and sundry others who have been aware of the vital necessity for humor and who have used it appropriately in the pulpit and out. But consider what it must have been like to listen to the Rev. Jonathan Edwards hour after hour! Or even to more modern evangelists.

Atheists are necessarily humorists

Unconscious humor abounds, among the liberal and the orthodox alike. For example, I once told a new friend from New Orleans that I assumed that he was a Roman Catholic.

"Oh no, Janx," he replied, "I'm an atheist, thank God!" But he smiled at the same time I did.

Omniscience required

On the other hand, one of my Kentucky great-grandfathers, a Presbyterian minister, was much given to wholly impromptu prayer. One of his difficulties was that his adjurations sometimes were obscure and convoluted to the point that he was not sure that even an omniscient deity could comprehend them. On an historic occasion, his language became so highly involved, with intricate construction and piled-up parentheses befogging his intentions, that he said, "In other words, O Lord," and started all over again.

Information cheerfully supplied

One common ministerial tendency in an earlier day was giving the Almighty the low-down, adding candle-power to His enlightenment.

The county's school teachers had assembled in a small Ohio town and the local Methodist minister felt that he should acknowledge their presence from his pulpit. He therefore prayed, "And send down Thy choicest blessings on the teachers of this land! Thou knowest, O Lord, that ninety-four and sixty-eight one-hundredths percent of them are women!"

Holy water: its manufacture and use

Bishop Irving Johnson of the Episcopal diocese of Colorado had arranged to baptize all seven of Pete Snedekor's grandchildren at Pete's Denver home on a pleasant August afternoon. The two were warm friends and Pete attempted to needle the Bishop about the probable inadequacy of his supply of holy water.

"My dear boy," said the Bishop, "if I find that my provision of holy water is indeed lacking, I am quite ready to prepare an appropriate quantity here and now."

"But, Bishop, how *do* you make holy water?"

"Quite simple to the initiated. You take plain tap-water, just plain, ordinary tap-water. And then you boil the Hell out of it!"

Bishop Johnson was a vigorous and sharply outspoken low-churchman. "Yes," he said, "these Episcopal clergymen who want to dress like Mother and be called Father!"

Instantaneous Group Conversion

The Bishop served for several years as chairman of Colorado's parole board. After nondenominational services in the state prison chapel, he said that he would be glad to confer privately in the warden's office with any of the inmates who happened to be Episcopalians. He asked, out of natural curiosity, "How many of you men *are* Episcopalians?"

Every hand in the room was raised.

"Ah," said the Bishop. "Now I know why we see so few men in our Sunday congregations here in Colorado!"

———

In the era when the Packard was America's acknowledged deluxe automobile, Mrs. Johnson once declared firmly to the Bishop, "Irving, I want you to know that I have my heart set on a Packard."

"My dear," he responded. "That is the only part of your anatomy that will ever 'set' on a Packard."

Religious liberals ride with the punch

Unitarians, standing with their Universalist friends on the left of the liberal wing of American churches, have been fair game for jibes of the more orthodox: the alleged prayer "To Whom It May Concern" and much more. But the best Unitarian quips come from members of that fellowship. For example, Pierre Van Passen remarked, "Yes, I belong to the Unitarian Church, where the only time anybody ever hears about Jesus is when the janitor falls down stairs."

That isn't so! Reverence is only a little less characteristic of Unitarian-Universalist churches than it is of the evangelistic variety. At least, reverence is extended to the other man's reverences, if not always to the object he reveres. But how could any sensitive person who has read the New Testament fail to revere Jesus of Nazareth? Or, shall we say, St. Francis of Assisi? Or the late, beneficent Pope John XXIII? Or who could read, and read smilingly, this inscription above the entrance to a mighty edifice beside the Potomac:

> IN THIS TEMPLE
> AS IN THE HEARTS OF THE PEOPLE
> FOR WHOM HE SAVED THE UNION
> THE MEMORY OF ABRAHAM LINCOLN
> IS ENSHRINED FOREVER

Serene, gentle humor

The gentle humor of kindly spirits once had, and still should have, its place. For example, Dr. John Allan Blair, long-time Presbyterian minister in Philadelphia and in Chambersburg, Pennsylvania, felt highly unconventional when he quoted a young friend as saying, "My girl is like brown sugar: sweet, but unrefined!" And when George Howard Bruce of the Horace Mann School flubbed an iron shot, he might say, "Peanuts!" But when he missed a 12-inch putt, he was known to exclaim hotly, "*Double* peanuts!"

Snickersnees at the alert

John Hendrikley and Tom Pasternall were close friends in their freshman year at a distinguished institution, but athletic and other internecine rivalries brought embitterment and they loathed each other by the time they were graduated.

John entered the service of his Church, Tom the Navy, and when they met from time to time, brief glares provided the only sign of recognition. Thirty years passed. John had become a Monsignor, Tom an Admiral. And they came face to face at the information desk in Grand Central Station, John in full sacerdotal vestments, Tom neat and trim, his uniform jacket bright with decorations.

"I must speak to this man," said John to himself. "As a matter of conscience, I simply must." So he took a step forward and inquired, "Conductor, when does the next train leave for Cincinnati?"

Tom was fully aware of his rival's ample figure

as he replied, "Madam, no woman in your condition should even dream of traveling!"

That third Sunday after Epiphany

The Rt. Rev. George Nuflo, bishop of an Episcopal diocese in New England, was one of the mighty malapropists of his day. Several of his performances became legendary, but none of them quite equaled this half-century-ago announcement:

"My dear friends, I am pleased to inform you that at our service on January 28th, the third Sunday after Epiphany, it will be my proud privilege to confer upon a large and splendid class the holy and apostolic rite of circumcision."

The devil and the evangelized

In one of Arkansas's smaller towns, a crowded evangelical meeting approached its climax. The minister, beating a tattoo on his pulpit, was evoking the sulphurous fumes of Hell itself when one of the young men of the community, filled with gin and iniquity, appeared at the church door clad in a complete Mephistopholes costume—bright red, horns, tail, and a small pitchfork. As can be imagined, the congregation went away from there, through doors, windows, the sides of the church.

Only an aging granny, badly crippled by rheumatism, was left to deal with his Satanic Majesty, who strode down the aisle, stopped at granny's pew and glowered.

"Mistah Devil," came her quavering voice, "I suppose they tol' you how ah comes here and sings the hymns and says the prayers. And that's true, Mistah Devil. Ah done done that. But Mistah Devil, ah wants y' t' know that, way down deep, ah always been on *yo'* side!"

Sam, the snake, the flea

Sam Jones, exciting Methodist evangelist of the late 19th century, was conducting a street-corner service in Dallas, Texas. Sam was avowedly a Georgia cracker and the crowd was subjecting him to good-natured twitting on the point. Someone finally asked, "Sam, what *is* the difference between a Georgia cracker and a Texan?"

"Why, I should say, suh, about the same as the difference between a snake and a flea!"

"I'll bite. What is the difference between a snake and a flea?"

"Well you see, suh, a snake crawls on his own belly. But a flea, he ain't so particular!"

Gamblers can be useful

"Parson" Simpkins, pastor of the First Congregational Church of Salt Lake City sixty years ago, was liberal far beyond his time. For example, at least once each week-end he informed participants in the traditional poker game which began at the Alta Club on Saturday noon that they were playing the next hand for his Sunday School. And all cards were consistently bet for what they were worth, but Simpkins scooped up the pot.

In March, 1898, Parson Simpkins met one of Salt Lake's professional gamblers, Henry McKimball, on Main Street and was told, "Parson, I've been lucky. And I have $500 right here in my hand I would like to give to your church. But this is gamblin' money, Parson. You may not want to take it."

The Parson reached instantly for Henry's currency. "My son," he said, "that money has been working for the Devil long enough. Time it went to work for the Lord!"

RACONTEUR EXTRAORDINARY

Paramount among the many raconteurs I have known is the late Joel L. Priest of Boise, Idaho, and Henderson, Kentucky. He practiced law briefly in Henderson, served as that community's municipal judge for one term, helped to cover the Chicago World's Fair of 1893 as a reporter for the long-defunct CHICAGO HERALD, *was editor and publisher of Henderson's daily, the* GLEANER, *went broke, moved out to Salt Lake City, Utah, to become star reporter, city editor and finally editor, of the* SALT LAKE HERALD. *Then after that newspaper died of a merger, he went to Boise, Idaho, as General Agent and political factotum of the Union Pacific Railroad. As a newspaperman in Salt Lake, he was responsible for reporting significant news the moment it developed anywhere in the far West: the Goldfield mining strike, the trial of Heywood, Moyer and Pettibone for the assassination of Governor Steunenberg of Idaho, and the 42-round, Gans-Nelson fight to a finish were examples. And he was on a train for San Francisco within two hours after word of the 1906 fire and earthquake reached Salt Lake.*

Joel was the Rocky Mountain area's favorite toastmaster. The gamut ran from the annual banquet of Idaho's undertakers to a dinner in honor of a foreign mission interested in irrigation practices.

His touch was always light; his impertinences never offended; his sense of appositeness was remarkable; his stories sparkled; his introductions were strictly limited to three minutes; he unhesitatingly cut off at the hips any gaseous speaker who blatted on beyond the time assigned to him. He loved a salty tale (many of the specimens in my collection are his), but he never told in public a story that was even mildly maculate.

If Joel ever was worsted in an exchange of repartee, the episode was not recorded, at least to my knowledge. The local wits, because of personal experience or on hearsay evidence, left him scrupulously alone. He was a good and gay companion. His sons, Joel, Jr., and A. J. have testified that they enjoyed their father's company more than that of any contemporary. If any modern scions can make that same statement (Joel, Jr. and A. J. are beyond retirement age), I will cheerfully buy them a full-page display in the CHARLOTTESVILLE DAILY PROGRESS.

Joel was my second cousin and I had known him intimately up to the day of his death. I loved him and rejoiced in him.

The treat and the necktie

In the early 1880's, Joel's mother gave him fifty cents to buy a necktie for himself, but he assembled his boon companions of those Henderson, Kentucky days, Phil Smith and Singleton and Lambert Kimmel (older brothers of Admiral Husband Kimmel, who was so unjustifiably pilloried after Pearl Harbor), bought a ten-cent treat for each member of the group and came home wearing a ten-cent tie.

Claims should be prompt

In his Chicago days, Joel had returned to Henderson for a week's vacation and went quail hunting with Phil Smith and Singleton Kimmel. They flushed a covey promptly and Joel, who had not used a shotgun in pre-Capone Chicago, fired away wildly and futilely with both barrels. The other two marksmen hit their birds and while they were still in the air, Joel exclaimed, "Goddlemighty, I got 'em both!"

Is anybody here?

When Joel came back from Chicago to Henderson, Kentucky, to become editor and publisher of the Henderson *Gleaner,* his ideas were slightly on the advanced side. For example, when it was announced that Sam Jones, a powerful evangelist who was the Billy Sunday or Billy Graham of his time, was to conduct a series of meetings in the community and that a wooden tabernacle would be built for the purpose, Joel said firmly in his editorials that Sam's rabble-rousing style was not consonant with Henderson's cultural qualities, that its residents would find Sam's sermons repugnant and would stay away from his tabernacle in large numbers.

Joel's editorials were forwarded to Sam by his committee and were acknowledged acidly, but the tabernacle continued to rise. Furthermore, it was completed on time. The great night came. And Henderson really turned out. Its citizens occupied every seat, crowded the standing room, draped themselves over the rafters.

Joel was there, necessarily—to be sure—in his reportorial capacity. And a shock was in store for him. Sam strode to the pulpit, smiled as he looked over the packed tabernacle and inquired ringingly, "Priest, are you here?"

Joel felt that personal publicity might be undesirable.

Again, "Priest, are you here?"

The true newspaperman's aversion to conspicuousness controlled Joel's conduct.

Once more, "Priest, are you here?" No answer. Then, "Well, Priest, if you are here, r'ar up on your hind legs, you little skunk you, and see if you can see anybody!"

Ebernand's essence

George Madison Priest, Joel's younger brother and the family scholar, went to Princeton. His Ph.D. thesis, "The Essence of Ebernand Von Erfurt," appeared between boards and finally reached the *Salt Lake Herald,* which Joel was then serving as city editor. Within days, a review was prepared, set in type and a copy which plainly seemed to have been clipped from the *Herald* of May 10, 1905, was forwarded to Princeton. It was scathing: "This pseudo-scholar has no spiritual affinity with Ebernand Von Erfurt or with any of that author's master works. His self-serving declaration that he has extracted Von Erfurt's 'essence' will seem blabbered nonsense to a competent critic. Has Priest read Von Erfurt in the original or has he examined no more than excerpts crudely translated by a Trenton, New Jersey, high school boy?" And much more.

Few practical jokes are amusing and this one may not have been, but George was a shade pedantic at the time, although he became genial and nonportentous in his later career. In any event, there was measurable coolness between the brothers for long months.

Move that car!

When Joel first came to Boise, Idaho, and the Union Pacific, he was given space with Frank Plaisted, later a major executive of the Southern Pacific. Plaisted occupied an inner and Joel an outer office. Joel always arrived first and when Plaisted put in his appearance, this colloquy became ritualistic:

"God morning, boss."

"Good morning, men. Is the car on the track?"

"Yes, boss, the car's on the track."

"Well, take it off! By God, I'll show you who's boss!"

One doubts that there is such an exchange each morning between the President and the Executive Vice President of Morgan Guaranty Trust Company.

The gift of prescience

Frank Plaisted came to his Salt Lake City desk one morning in the '90's to be told that a daughter just born to one of his associates had arrived with a thin, diaphonous membrane known as a "caul" over her eyes and that a child so born had the gifts of prescience, of prevision, of foresight.

Plaisted replied at once that he was sure that he had come equipped with a caul over his ass, because his hindsight was so much better than his foresight!

Hospitality and the shepherd

In his youthful days, Joe Plaisted, Frank's brother, ran a flock of sheep, operating in the high hills with the usual campwagon. One afternoon a stranger appeared, black with grime and gamy enough to repel even the hardiest mosquito. The custom of the country required that bed and board be furnished to any such wayfarer, but Plaisted sought escape.

"My friend," he said, "I would like to be able to put you up tonight, but I just can't do it. You see, I'm lousy."

"Hell, don't let that bother you none, partner. I'm lousy, too!"

Tenors and tremors

One of Joel's many stories about the San Francisco disaster involved Enrico Caruso, who was in his tub at the Palace Hotel when the earthquake struck. The great tenor draped himself in a towel and rushed into the street. Then, as he encountered the cool night air, the ruling passion of his life overcame him. He sang, "Mi, mi, mi!" and wrapped the towel around his golden throat.

Regurgitated laughter

Boise, Idaho, had been a branch line town for 50 years. The junction point was Nampa, where a 20-mile trip to the state's capital was begun. Then in 1921, after prolonged negotiations, the Union Pacific looped its main line through Boise, to the community's exhilarated satisfaction.

In that same year, Joel had attended a service club dinner. The toastmaster, Rosey Roseman, was in bad form that night. Diffuse and drivelous, Rosey pointed to Joel and said, "You down there, Col. Priest, we have needed this main line in Boise a long time! When I first came to Boise, they kicked me off the train at Nampa at half-past three in the morning. Think of that, Col. Priest, kicked me off the train at Nampa at half-past three in the morning!"

Joel's reply came instantaneously: "But Rosey, you should have ridden a passenger train."

The crowd roared, thought a moment, and then guffawed again, the only regurgitated laugh in my long experience.

As Maine goes

I had come back to Boise for a visit just after the early 1932 election in which Maine had gone Democratic for the first time since the Civil War.

OH—8

The Priests brought old friends together in my honor. And politics entered the conversation.

Joel had retained the Democratic predilections of his Kentucky youth, while I had become a Republican. Naturally enough, Joel called on me for an explanation of the Maine result and I could come up with no more than highly fictitious statistics about prevalent illiteracy among Maine's citizens.

"I can believe that, Janx," Joel replied. "I really can believe that. That's why they have been Republicans so long!"

The completely accepted lobbyist

Joel had acknowledged status as the principal lobbyist for the Union Pacific Railroad before the Idaho Legislature. He was Speaker of the Third House, as well as permanent chairman of the Committee on Interference and Obstruction, and defeat came to him rarely.

It was one of Joel's techniques to approach a group of heads-together, buzzing legislators and inquire, "Anything confidential about this, boys?" The almost invariable reply was, "Not at all, Joel, not at all." And Joel would declare, "Then to Hell with it! I'm not interested," and walk away. It was always good for a laugh.

Taxis and friendship

Boise knew Joel by his first name and he ordinarily could respond in kind. One day his taxi-operating friend, Pete Landstrop, was driving him over to the State Capitol when an elderly citizen hesitated in front of the car and just made the sidewalk with a quick jump.

"That was Senator Henry Bottomley," Joel observed. "He's the worst enemy I have in the State Senate."

"Hell, why didn't you tell me, Joel?" Pete responded. "I could'a got him easy!"

There stood General Washington

Joel said that this tale was told him by his father, who had it, in turn (this *is* still a young country), from an actual auditor:

Jabez Gowdy, who had served in General Washington's forces as a sutler for three months, but who promoted himself to colonel for the benefit of the next generation, was relating his exploits at the battle of Trenton.

"It was toward the end of a terrible day," he said, "when I suddenly found myself deserted and alone. My dastardly aide had escaped, taking with him the tattered remnants of my regiment and I realized that the red-coats were upon me.

Fortunately, however, I stood at the narrow eastern ford of Micosa creek. And, my friends, I stood.

"On came the enemy, but my flashing sabre made 'em pause. Again they advanced. And I most solemnly assure you that I cut and I parried and I thrust and I hewed and I hacked and I slashed until before me lay a veritable mound of British dead.

"Then I felt a light touch upon my shoulder. I turned and there stood General Washington. I shall never forget the majesty of his demeanor and the solemnity of his tone as he said, 'Colonel, for God's sake stay your hand! Would you turn the battlefield into a slaughter house?'"

Swept sand and the Elks

Joel's sprightly and engaging wife, Sue, was less than enthusiastic about the Benevolent and Protective Order of Elks, to which her spouse gave time and attention.

"Oh, my dear," said Joel after a mild argument, "please remember that 'The faults of our brothers we write upon the sands; their virtues are engraved upon the everlasting tablets of love and memory.'"

"Can't be done," Sue insisted.

"Why not?"

"Not enough sand!"

Elks and exaltation

Sue Priest, whose ardor for two-legged Elks was dilute, was told by her gregarious husband, Joel, that he had to forego a second cup of coffee and hurry to the railroad station to help greet the Elks' Grand Exalted Ruler, who was making a brief stop. "I'm coming with you," Sue immediately replied. "I *am* coming with you. I never have seen an exalted Elk."

The great Kibitzer

Joel happened to be in our Wall Street law offices when General Dwight D. Eisenhower was given his triumphal, torn-paper reception by the financial district. Surrounded by some of our young women, who consistently made a pet of him, Joel observed, as he looked down on packed humanity which occupied every available square foot of space, "Girls, I wouldn't get into that crowd to watch the Twelve Apostles play pinochle."

"Come, come, Joel," I said, "don't be sacrilegious."

"You listen to me, Janx!" was his answer. "I wouldn't get into that crowd to watch the Twelve Apostles play pinochle, even if the Holy Ghost was kibitzing!"

Beer and buttermilk

Joel Priest and I were seated in a dining car, en route to Pocatello, Idaho, when that state was enmeshed in the 1916 campaign which put a bone-dry clause into its constitution. The citizen opposite us might have posed for Enright's comic figure of Old Man Prohibition: funeral vestments, black tie, heavy jowls, fingernails in mourning, the lowering scowl of a bilious undertaker. He had asked for buttermilk, while Joel ordered beer. And when the two potations were served, he inquired sourly, "Don't you like buttermilk?" "No!" Joel replied, "I don't like buttermilk. But, by God, I'm not trying to pass any laws to keep you from drinking it!"

Rhetoric among the sagebrush

In a chamber-of-commerce mood, Joel once declaimed, "Idaho is the land of sagebrush and sunshine, of optimism and opportunity, where the desert has been made to bloom like the rose and where the weird wailing of the coyote has been metamorphosed into the laughter of happy children in many contented homes.

"Yes, Idaho! If all the white pines in Idaho were one white pine, its topmost boughs would brush small stars from out the Milky Way! If all the purebred sheep in Idaho were one sheep, its all-pervasive bleating would awaken sleepers upon distant Mars. And if all the perfect baking potatoes in Idaho were one potato, it would take one thousand men one hundred years to peel it and the peeling would encircle the globe seven and one-quarter times."

En route from Salt Lake City to Chicago, Joel, Jr., tried that language on the gentle Bishop Hopson of the Episcopal Church. The Bishop smiled faintly and observed, "O my! How quaintly sophomoric!"

Humor that is kindly

Joel's humor was occasionally sharp, but the sting was only momentary. He said that it was much more difficult to be funny and kind than to evoke laughter through another's humiliation. And at least in public, he was unfailingly kind. Given a larger stage, he might have challenged the incomparable Will Rogers. In all events, his memory will remain green in the vast land that extends westward from the Rockies to the Pacific.

Great White Register

His southern accent quite gone, Joel was of the West. And yet sentimental ties to Henderson,

Kentucky, persisted. This was the peroration of a talk made before the Henderson Rotary Club in the 1930's: "And when the time comes for me to write my name upon the Great White Register, it shall be there inscribed as 'Joel L. Priest of Henderson, Kentucky.'" Perhaps Henderson *and* Boise, Idaho, can claim him. There was enough of him for both.

HERE A HODGE, THERE A PODGE

Call this section miscellaneous, heterogeneous: what you will. The stories it contains were set down as they have been recalled and, except for the fictionalization of certain names, quite as they happened in my presence or were told me by observant friends. There has been no attempt at classification. Not even chronology would be a useful guide. They are not intended to be either moral or amoral. My target is the solar plexus.

Between syllables

Bill Dawson, Cleveland lawyer, law professor and soldier, quite ruptured the dignity of the old Greenbrier dining room when, in the early 20's he gave me this account of the most profane man in Ohio, one Peter Glomford, superintendent of a woodworking establishment at Akron.

Pete's speech finally became so heavily interlarded with expletives that he could find satisfaction only by cursing between syllables. Upbraiding an employee at the top of his powerful voice, he declared, "See here, feller. You're gettin' entirely too inde-God-damn-pendent around the joint. Pretty soon you'll be havin' the idea that *you're* the superin-God-damn-tendent of this plant yourself!"

That feuhrer principle

In the mid-'30's, when Nazism was being hailed as the Wave of the Future, a certain Dr. Wilhelm Wagner served as cultural attaché to the German consulate in Cleveland. He was making real progress, especially among members of college faculties in the area who had studied at German universities, when he made an appointment with Professor Bill Dawson at Bill's suburban home.

When Wagner arrived, Bill had just completed the hiving of a swarm of bees. The new queen bee had been fully accepted by her loyal subjects and Wagner remarked, "Ah, Herr Professor Dawson, that is a magnificent demonstration of the feuhrer principle in nature!"

Bill paused dramatically for 20 seconds before he replied, "I'll be interested in a feuhrer when you show me one who can lay eggs!"

Dr. Wagner executed an abrupt about-face. He did not look back. Nor did he remain long in Cleveland.

Prunes: eighty cents a portion

Frank Kerr of Butte, Montana, was staying in the old Belmont Hotel, a then elegant establishment near Grand Central in New York. The year was 1928 and Italian prunes were selling for 50 cents a hundred-weight in Montana's Missoula valley.

Kerr, who was strongly far-sighted, had come down to breakfast without his glasses, and was holding the menu at arm's length. He finally beckoned a waiter and said, "Prunes. I want some prunes."

The waiter gracefully indicated an item with his pencil and said, "There you are, sir. Prunes: eighty cents a portion."

"Eighty cents!" yelled Kerr. "Eighty cents! Why, you son-of-a-bitch, you can't *carry* eighty cents worth of prunes!"

Pachydermous dexterity

Clem Holding of Raleigh, North Carolina, tells about the escape, unnoticed and in the early morning, of the sole elephant rejoiced in by a circus playing a small North Carolina town. There had been no trace of the pachyderm until a distraught woman living outside the community called its chief of police. "Officer," she said, "there's a great, huge animal out in my garden pulling up all my vegetables with its tail." "Pulling up your vegetables?" the chief asked. "What's he doing with 'em?" "Oh officer, officer," was the reply, "if I told you, you just wouldn't believe me!"

Giddap, mule

Claudius N. Sapp, who became a successful South Carolina lawyer, decided as a farm boy of 17 that farming was not the occupation for a young man of his aptitudes and abilities. He was plowing one day with a mule, came to the end of his furrow, dropped the traces, and declared, "I ain't nevah again in my whole life goin' to say 'Giddap' to no mule—not even if the son-of-a-bitch sits in my lap!"

What would you say?

The late and unconventional Pierce Butler, Jr., of St. Paul, was filling out an application for life insurance which contained this question: "Do you take alcoholic liquors in any form?"

Pierce's answer was accurate and unequivocal: "In any form!"

The retort gentle

The small driver of a Model A Ford, his mind on other considerations, crashed into the rear of a ten-ton truck. No serious damage was done, but a burly neanderthal climbed down from the truck, surveyed the scene and began to discuss the little driver's ancestry from the primeval ooze upward.

He finally paused, out of breath. Plainly annoyed because there had been no rejoinder, he said, "Cat got y'r tongue, fella? Ain't ya gonna speak up? Ain't ya gonna call me nothin'?"

The little man licked his dry lips, gulped and replied, "Well, I was thinkin' of calling you a bastard. But you don't look like no love child to me!"

Best terms for actors

Abner Anxsman, proprietor of the Augusta Hotel in Augusta, Maine, in the 1890's, had been consistently bilked by traveling thespians who had taken advantage of his hospitality and decamped in the dark of the moon. His opinion of that entire profession was, therefore, low.

Then an obvious wearer of the buskin stood before Anxsman. He wore the stovepipe hat, the black tie, the funeral vestments. Thrusting a hand into his double-breasted coat, he inquired patronizingly, "My good man, what are your best terms —your very best terms—for actors?"

"My best terms for actors? My best terms for actors! Bastards and sons-of-bitches!"

Music can be apposite

In the second decade of these 100 years, Sam Ingrall, the proprietor of Moscow, Idaho's, only motion-picture palace, doubled as its violinist. Films were silent ("One minute to change reels, please") and music which occasionally proved apposite was provided by Sam and his wife, the latter doing her best at a battered upright piano.

Louise Glaum, one of the less conspicuous vampires of the time, had shattered five or six lives. But the nemesis that always awaited such servants of Satan finally descended upon her. And as she staggered into the purple sunset to die, Sam and Mrs. Sam played "The End of a Perfect Day."

———

This came from Verna J. at about the time it happened:

Just as Kaiser Wilhelm was establishing himself in Holland after World War I, France sent to this country Mme. Heloise Damont, who had been brilliantly effective in arranging entertainments—some of them near the front lines—which helped to sustain the morale of General Pershing's young men. Every effort was made to extend proper hospitality and, among other things, the lady was told that she could meet anyone she pleased, even including President Wilson.

"Later, but not at once," she said. "First—first of all—I must embrace your magnificent Mme. Abitch, who sent so many of her splendid sons to save France!"

The eye-witness

In Columbia, South Carolina, just as this century dawned, I made the acquaintance of Major Abner Doubledark, who had served gallantly under General Gordon and who was altogether willing to narrate his experiences after a single drink. The Confederacy was made to live again: alike for him and for his auditors.

At a modest gathering of young and old, the Major was asked to tell several mere Northerners about the battle of Sand Ridge, which had been fought just outside Columbia in the Spring of 1864.

"Well, suh," he began, "Sand Ridge was an outstandin' example of Confederate valor, of heroic determination, in th' face of odds that would have made a Yankee face turn cardboard gray.

"They had formed on th' northern side of the ridge and they were three to our one. What's mo', they had new carbines at their shoulders; their unifo'ms were some dirty, but not even patches on 'em; they had been eatin' regular and frequent; and they all had shoes.

"Whilst arrayed south of th' ridge were th' embattled fo'ces of the Confederacy. We had old coon-huntin' rifles in our hands; we had just one meal of co'n-pone th' day befo'; our unifo'ms were in tatters; and our feet were bound in rags. But

I would have you know, suh, that so fired and inspired were we by our zeal for our great and righteous cause that we swept them Yankees befo' us like chaff, suh!"

From a corner came the protesting voice of another veteran, "But, Major, that ain't quite right. I fit the battle of Sand Ridge too. I fit not ten feet from you. Them damn Yankees was too many fo' us that day. They run us down the valley about ten mile."

The Major exhaled a deep sigh. "Ah," he said. "Another perfectly good story ruined by a damned eyewitness!"

Earn a gold watch

When Claude N. Sapp, who was to become United States District Attorney in Columbia, South Carolina, was a farm boy, he fell for one of those advertisements in an agricultural weekly which urged youths to "sell 36 packages of our bluing at ten cents a package and earn a handsome gold watch."

"I sent for them packages," he reported in the country talk he loved. "And I sold 'em amongst the neighbors, mostly a nickel down and a nickel subsequently. But when them folks told me to turn in the money, it had oozed away.

"I didn't dare ask my Daddy for it, because he

was a hard-shelled Baptist and he would have skun me alive. And them letters kept gettin' meaner and tougher. They had me right in the jail house and prayin' didn't seem to help so much.

"Finally I got a letter from 'em that I knew just by its smell was nastier and ornerier than any of the others. So I sat down in the postoffice and I took out a little stub pencil and I wrote across the back of that envelope, 'Claude Sapp is dead. Jacob Galloway, Postmaster.' And it went back. And you know, I still owe them fellers that $3.60."

Sovereign power

Humor out of the movement toward world order and decency is necessarily rare. It isn't easy to be funny about the alternative: mankind fricasseed in a nuclear flame-out.

In all events, the Rev. Fr. Edward J. Conway, S.J., spoke on planetary wholeness under law before a Chicago audience some years ago. And, after his talk, he found himself surrounded by a group of Coughlinites and other readers of a newspaper difficult to recall by name. One of them finally seized Conway by the coat lapels and said fiercely, "We know what you want us to do, Father. We know what you want us to do! You want us to surrender our sovereignginity!"

The deficiencies of translation

Abraham Wilson, attending an outdoor performance of *King Lear,* was stopped in the course of the first intermission by an elderly woman who sought directions to a nearby streetcar line. Wilson asked why the inquirer was not seeing the performance through, to be informed: "My dear, I saw it forty years ago in Yiddish and, frankly, it loses something in translation!"

I know him myself

Robert Halliday, executive vice president of a major New York City bank, was to be one of several speakers at a large Philadelphia banquet. He exchanged the normal mumbling, mutually unintelligible identification with the man on his right and finally was introduced at some length. His neighbor turned as the effusiveness proceeded and observed, "I hope that son-of-a-bitch Halliday won't talk too long!"

"He won't," Halliday replied, pushing back his chair. "I know the son-of-a-bitch well."

Enough time

Judge Ainsworth Monctoby had come back to Henderson, Kentucky, from Cambridge in the early 1890's with a law degree and a Harvard accent. One of them could be forgiven (he did serve a term on the municipal bench), but not both.

Conspirators, including Orwood Marshall and Henry McReynolds, made arrangements with a young man who was about to leave town for strictly personal reasons. The clock in the tower of the county building was about to strike once to designate 2:30 when this lad knocked at the Judge's office door.

"Good afternoon, son. What can I do for you?"

"Please be kind enough, if y' don't mind, suh, to tell me the correct time."

The judge removed his turnip-sized gold watch from a vest pocket: "Why it is exactly hawf-pawst two."

"Well, suh, at hawf-pawst three, you can kiss my awss!"

The youth sprinted down the hall with Monctoby in hot pursuit, took a single flight of stairs three at a time and disappeared into the warm August afternoon.

Of course the conspirators were on hand. "Why, Judge," asked Marshall with deep concern. "What can possibly be the trouble?"

"That b-bawstard," the Judge gasped. "That b-bawstard said I could kiss his awss at hawf-pawst three."

"But why be in such a hell of a hurry? You've got a whole hour!"

Was it Jacob's coat?

Electric Bond and Share Company was preparing an annual report and, in the first draft, S. Z. Mitchell, then boss of the ranch, had referred to Jacob's coat of many colors. E. B. Lee, the company statistician, made the appropriate change to Joseph, Mitchell went back to Jacob, then Lee to Joseph, for five or six proofs.

I happened to be in the Old Man's office one afternoon when Lee brought in the latest galleys, to be glared at sternly by Mitchell. "Lee," he announced, "I said 'Jacob' and I mean 'Jacob.' Now let it alone!"

"I'm sorry, Mr. Mitchell," Lee replied, "but it was Joseph who had the coat of many colors. Jacob was celebrated for his ladder, don't you remember?"

"Get a Bible!" the Old Man ordered.

Somebody at Two Rector Street managed to come up with a copy of the King James version and Lee turned to Joseph's story in the Book of Genesis. Mitchell read it, looked up at Lee, down at the Bible, up at Lee.

"Lee," he finally demanded, "are you Goddam sure you've got the right edition?"

All the best

When the eastern California mining camp of Nehri was being developed in the 1880's, its most vigorous promoter was George Salisbury, who had been a brigadier general in the Union army and who left his family in Boston for five years as the new community was being shaped. In that interim, the general had taken an attractive squaw as his companion. Mrs. Salisbury and the children did not appear until Nehri had achieved many of civilization's concomitants, including a Methodist church. Within a week, Mrs. Salisbury became the guest at a meeting of the Ladies Aid Society and routine business was disposed of promptly so that she could be told, in shocked whispers, about the general's inamorata.

Mrs. Salisbury was sharply taken aback, but she rallied to reply with Bostonian calm: "You know, ladies, I can believe that. I really can believe that. The general always was one to demand the very best the community affords!"

Tom-cats and moose-heads

Two from North Carolina:

The George Hallmans of Raleigh had an aged but virile tom-cat named Oscar, great lover and superb feline baritone. Oscar's popularity in the neighborhood finally became so dilute that the Hallmans consented to an operation. Oscar was altered; in Mrs. Hallman's phrase, his "hem was let down."

The neighborhood was quiet for some days, but the very night Oscar was released from durance, pandemonium exploded. And Oscar was in the middle of it all, howling his noblest solos. When Hallman complained sharply to the veterinarian next day, that worthy replied, "Please understand, Mr. Hallman, that old Oscar was acting purely in a' advisory capacity."

———

Among George Hallman's office assets were a large moose-head and an inquisitive secretary who was particularly curious as to how he came by it. After having been asked about the head on various occasions, George said with some exasperation, "All right, Miss Myopia, I'll tell you the story. I was fishing in Maine eight years ago and was walking back to camp with nothing to show for my efforts. The mosquitoes were terrible, so I was carrying a bottle of turpentine to keep 'em away. I had no gun—just my fishing pole—so I had to run when that big lug of a moose charged me. And I put a pine tree between us. He stopped, puffed and ran me around the tree three or four times. I just managed to stay ahead of him and then I had an idea. I pulled out my handkerchief, rolled it into a ball, soaked it in turpentine, and when he charged again I sprinted and almost caught up with him.

"Well, his tail was up. So I threw my turpentined handkerchief and I shot a bull's-eye. I don't expect you to believe this, Miss Myopia, but when that moose finished sliding up and down the gravelly river bottom, that head was all there was left of him!"

Hindemith in North Carolina

Henry, the teen-age son of a North Carolina friend, was making some progress with his violin when he was given a piece by Hindemith. The music was difficult, Henry was slaughtering it, and the family pooch, Bosco, began to howl dolefully and dismally. The head of the family endured this duet through ten full minutes before he entreated, "Henry, for God's sake, play something that Bosco doesn't know!"

That previous question

Almost 25 years ago, the late Edgar H. Dixon, who was to be pilloried in the United States Senate with no trace of justification, had just been elected president of Middle South Utilities. Confronted with his first stockholders' meeting, he was worried about parliamentary procedure. Bill Staplin and A. J. Priest therefore spent three hours with him in an effort to provide at least the rudiments. As they were about to leave his office, Priest asked, a bit sharply, "Edgar, what would you do if I were to leap up in the rear row tomorrow morning and shout, 'I move the previous question!'?"

Without a moment's hesitation, Edgar replied, "I would say, 'You little red-headed son-of-a-bitch back there, you sit down!' "

Only technically flawed.

Parliamentary elegance

The secretary-treasurer of a San Francisco longshoremen's union was one Tony Gaspelli, nosy, a busybody, a pest. Tony had been making himself especially obnoxious at the monthly meeting when a harsh voice came from the rear of the room, "Maka d' mosh' Tony Gaspelli is beeg som'beech!"

Tony at once picked on a smaller citizen and asked, "You maka d' mosh'?" "No, Tony Gaspelli. I no maka d' mosh'." Another little man was interrogated, with the same result, and then a huge longshoreman stood up, pounded his barrel-like chest and declared, "Me, Tony Gaspelli! I maka d' mosh'!"

Tony wheeled toward the chairman with his hand upraised, "Second d' mosh'!"

Making an impression

Some years ago, a young woman in Wichita Falls, Texas, had permitted herself certain relaxations not altogether of the spirit on a flat tombstone in the local cemetery. The next morning she had a distressing backache and said to her sister, "Lucinda, m' back feels like it's come in two. Look and see if it ain't broke." After an appropriate examination, Lucinda replied, "No, Mary Lou, y' back ain't broke, but yo' ass done died on d' tent' of May, 1844!"

What are they for?

J. B. Thomas once told about the countryman who, on a visit to Fort Worth, found himself in a state of cruel constipation. One of his more sophisticated friends recommended glycerin suppositories, so he bought a bottle of them at 10:30 a.m., another at 12:00 noon and still another at 3:00 that afternoon. The salesman who had served him each time finally asked, "Mister, what have you been doing with these things? Have you been eating them, for Heaven's sake?"

"Of co's I been eatin' 'em", was the reply. "What the Hell did you think I was doin' with 'em —shovin' 'em up m' ass?"

Memory's lane

At a New York City banquet of the 1930's, I felt under obligation to introduce the diner on my right to the gentleman on his right, but the name had escaped, so I resorted to an ancient device. I put an affectionate hand on my friend's shoulder and asked, "Let's see, old timer, don't you spell your name in rather a peculiar way?"

The reply was harsh: "My name is Scott, S-C-O-T-T. How the Hell did you think I spelled it? With a 'Q'?"

Speakers and salt

Charles P. Taft, who had just been introduced with excessive fervor, told about a certain Ethel Oskins, whose one novel had become a best-seller and who was greatly sought after as a speaker before women's clubs.

On one occasion, Ethel was presented gushingly, frothily, by the club chairman, Mamie Morton-Gordon, and was quite flustered when she rose to speak. "Please, please, dear ladies," she said.

"You must not accept all of Mrs. Morton-Gordon's utterances at their face value. You really should take whatever she says with just a little dose of salts!"

Canteloupes are a gamble

The complaint clerk at a large Bladeway store near Summit, New Jersey, had not been doing badly when an irate woman customer appeared bearing a cantaloupe.

"Mister," she said, "I bought two of these things, just alike, for 39 cents each yesterday afternoon. We tried one last night and it tasted like a pumpkin with liver complaint. We ain't touched this one and I want my dough for it right now!"

"Sorry! Exceedingly sorry! But we never make refunds on cantaloupes. As everyone should appreciate, they are a gamble. Satisfactory flavor cannot be guaranteed. Refund is quite out of the question."

"Then I'll tell you what you can do with this one! You can take it and shove it 'way—".

"Madam," the clerk interrupted, "you must await your turn like everyone else. There are two pineapples and an egg-beater ahead of you!"

Don't annoy no jackass

The 80-year-old state representative of a Virginia cooperative had been nagged, needled and harassed by the chairman of his organization's annual meeting until he felt required to take the floor.

"My good friends," he said. "I am reminded of my long-ago boyhood. We had a jackass on the family farm and it was fun to pester him until he got ornery. My brother and I found a hole in the barn and we used to poke that jackass with long sticks so he got all steamed up. When my father learned about it, he worked us over some and then said to me, 'Henry, pokin' that animal has got to stop. I'm tellin' you that the time is goin' to come when a jackass will haunt you.'

"Well, I somehow knew that time would come. But I didn't know it would be today."

Well, why not?

Mrs. John Jacob Astor, like many other patriotic women, helped entertain World War I soldiers. An attractive woman, she had been kind to many doughboys and one sought her name for future reference. She answered gently, "I am Mrs. John Jacob Astor." And the reply was "Chicken, when you fly: fly high!"

My new corporal's stripes

On my first tour of duty as corporal of the guard in World War I, I was required, among other things, to search the prisoners, one of whom was a tough little mug from the 1st Infantry, then at Camp Lewis. As the examination continued—slapping thighs, under arms and the rest—the little guy looked me over coldly and deliberately, noting especially the new corporal's stripes. Then he observed loudly, "They just don't *give* a good Goddam *what* they make corporal in this man's army any more, do they!"

That probably was an old army witticism, as I learned later, when Xenophon and his ten thousand marched to the sea. But ah, at the time!

Here is the formula

Pierce Butler, Jr., once gave me specific instructions guaranteed to determine whether a Texan was lying:

"Observe first the fine lines around his eyes, Janx," he said. "Then notice the back of his left hand and see if you can catch the throb or pulse of a vein or artery. Then look at his mouth. If it's open, he's lying!"

Breakfast in Augusta

Admiral Simms, who commanded our North Sea fleet in World War I, had as one of his staff liaison officers a British commander whose appreciation of the humorous was stolidly leaden. That ineptitude, be it said, was not and is not characteristic of his gallant nation. What *would* the world have done without William S. Gilbert? What American politician ever approached Winston Churchill's wit?

In all events, the commander said to Simms, "Now, Admiral, I appreciate your American jokes. I grasp the nub. I laugh at the proper time. Just try me!"

Simms responded by saying that, as a midshipman, he had appeared for breakfast in the dining room of the excellent and then American-plan Augusta House in Augusta, Maine, and had asked a waitress what was available. That young woman recited the entire menu, concluding with those New England breakfast specialties, mince pie, prune pie and apple pie.

The prospective admiral said, "I'll have oatmeal and corn meal and scrambled eggs and poached eggs and ham and bacon and scrapple and hot cakes and waffles and mince pie and prune pie."

Lifting her arms akimbo, the waitress asked, "Well, what the Hell's wrong with the apple pie?"

The commander's face remained wholly blank.

Then he inquired petulantly, "Well, Admiral, what *was* wrong with the apple pie?"

That wonderful Poland water

When the Brothers Ricker were operating the Poland Spring House in Maine, Hiram was approached one morning by an enthusiastic guest who said, "Mr. Ricker, I want you to know that I have just drunk eleven glasses of your marvelous Poland water!" "Yes, yes, madam," Hiram replied. "Don't let me detain you, madam."

Thank you, Junior League

For one who has stopped name-droppers with the inquiry, "Don't you know any of the worthy poor?" this rejection, by a thirty-four-and-one-half-years-old woman, of an invitation to join the Junior League, was satisfying. It must be remembered that Junior League membership is unattainable after one reaches her 35th birthday.

"I am indeed honored, and I am sorry, but my joining the Junior League now would be like pledging a sorority in graduation week," said our charmer. "Thanks. But no thanks."

Hold that question

When Donna Baker was five, she had a large doll. Aggressive visitors in her home, seeking to demonstrate special interest in the child, fired a series of questions.

"What is the doll's name? Perhaps I can guess. Is it Alice? Is it Elsie? Is it Gwendolyn? Is it Deborah?"

Donna compressed her lips in a firm line and ordered: "Keep quiet and I'll tell you."

Try it some time, brother

Rex Stout, possessor of what must be the most luxuriant, exotically lush beard in New York's literary circles, was deep in a forthcoming Nero Wolfe mystery as he drove well over the Merritt Parkway speed limit. When a Connecticut state trooper asked the usual, "Well, where do you think *you're* going?" Rex gulped and replied, "Officer, I was hurrying home to shave." The cop stifled inward laughter with a harsh, "Get the Hell outa' here!"

Gentle, but firm

One of the sweet souls of my broad acquaintance was George Howard Bruce, a deeply loved teacher at Horace Mann School for many years. George put me on my seat at least twice.

My hair flamed a bit before the gray dimmed its aura and his own follicular foliage was less than lush. So one day I said, "George, I guess you just weren't around when St. Peter was handing out the hair, were you?"

"Oh yes, Janx, my lad," he replied, "I was there. I was there. But all he had left was *red* hair!"

On still another occasion, the wedding of a close mutual friend, I said in George's presence to the Episcopal minister who performed the ceremony, "Doctor Brown, I hate to make this observation, but the fact is that Mr. Bruce is so completely, so thoroughly, orthodox that he actually believes in infant damnation."

Again a slow appraisal and a gentle smile. I *would,* Janx," he said, "if *you* were an infant!"

One from Will R.

So far as I know, this one has never been published. In any event, I heard Will Rogers, then playing in the Ziegfield Follies, offer it from the stage of the New Amsterdam roof in June, 1917.

"One of our chorus boys is stopped last week by a hatchet-faced woman patriot and she asks, 'Young man, why aren't you in the service of your country?'

"And he answers, 'Madam, for the same reason that you're not in the Ziegfield chorus: physical disability!'"

Brothers-in-law, not mothers-in-law, are fair game

Tom was dragging a dead horse down Market Street here in Charlottesville, Virginia, not many months ago. He was stopped by Sgt. Ray Clarity of our local police force. "In Heaven's name, what gives?" asked Ray.

"You know that damn', cocky smart-aleck brother-in-law of mine," Tom replied. "Well, he's always comin' to me and givin' me questions like this: 'Tom, did you know it was 25,000,000,000,000 miles to the nearest fixed star? Do you know the name of that there fixed star? Did you know that two separate guys named Adlai E. Stevenson has held high office in our great country? What was them offices?' I always says I don't know. And, Ray, I'm gettin' tired of it.

"So this time I fix him. I'm gonna drag this horse home. And I'm gonna haul him upstairs. And I'm gonna put him in the bath tub. And pretty quick my damn' brother-in-law will come runnin' down and he'll find me and ask me, all out of breath, 'Tom, did you know there was a big, dead horse upstairs in the bath tub?'"

"And I'm gonna look him over real slow. Then I'm gonna say, 'Yes, you dumb son-of-a-bitch, I *know!*' "

Sweet, gracious F. G. Cooper

I was having lunch, at least as far back as the early 1940's, with Clarence Streit and F. G. Cooper. Veterans will remember that F. G. C. once shared a sparkling page of the old *Collier's* with Grantland Rice, accompanying his delightful drawings with gentle humor.

I asked if he recalled his depicting of two hens, one of whom inquired, "Woman, why do you always lay your eggs hard-berlt?" The reply was, "I guess I take me bawth too hot!"

"No, Janx," Cooper replied, "I did thousands of those cartoons and I don't remember that one. But it *sounds like me.*"

Booth Tarkington was a raconteur

Chester Poole of Ivy, Virginia, says that he attended, in the Spring of 1901, a dinner given for Sir Henry Irving in the Green Room of a Chicago theater. Booth Tarkington was one of the guests and Chester recalls this as Tarkington's story for the occasion:

Father and son were driving a load of hay along one of Indiana's narrow roads when a jutting boulder careened load and riders into a deep ditch. The boy was thrown clear and he set out immediately for help from a nearby community.

He was received sympathetically at the local tavern and volunteers promised aid, but he was urged to refresh himself with a cup of coffee.

The young man accepted with some reluctance, saying, "Dad ain't gonna like this."

The ham sandwich and apple pie pressed upon him also disappeared, but with the reiterated observation, "Dad ain't gonna like this."

"But, son, why do you keep saying your father will object to our takin' care of you."

"Huh-uh, Dad ain't gonna like it. He's under the hay!"

THE FOURTH ESTATE

My affection for the ink-stained is not quite reverent, but will remain warm and strong to the final trump. They have always been underpaid and overworked. But they are the elect of our broad land. Just these few truthful tales—all from the West—to give them recognition.

Read 'em over, brother

The double-jointed word used carelessly is a major reportorial hazard, as was demonstrated on *The Salt Lake Tribune* one bad night when a half-completed press run had to be stopped, papers pulled back from the mail room, and a replate done on a sports page.

Anthony W. Ivins, first counselor in the First Presidency of the Church of Jesus Christ of Latter-day Saints, and one of the community's most admired citizens, had proved his soundness of wind and limb at age 80 by shooting a deer when the Utah season opened.

An excellent picture of President Ivins with his big game trophy appeared on page 6, but it carried this unfortunate caption: "Tony Ivins, despite his senility, bags his deer."

City editors sometimes make friends

Many years ago eight solemn men massed around the desk of a young reporter to watch the presentation of a tome of at least twenty pages. The leader warned: "This material must be used precisely as it is written here; it must not be changed."

The astounded reporter explained as politely as he could that the use of such material was the province of the city editor. And that worthy, attracted by the mob scene, came over.

"Mr. Lowry," the reporter reported, "these gentlemen insist that this material be printed as is."

Without glancing at the manuscript, the city editor tore it in two pieces, dropped them in a capacious waste basket, and inquired, with a quick bow:

"Is there anything else I can do for you gentlemen?"

Empathy at its tenderest

Gene Fowler, one of the more imaginative newspaper men of this century, was attempting to deprecate his reportorial skill. "I think I wasn't objective enough as a reporter," he said. "I was always putting myself in the other guy's place, which is why I finally had to give up covering hangings."

My husband! Ah, my husband!

World War II brought a labor shortage to Utah. The women came to the rescue, keeping both home and economic fires burning by taking the places in industry of their menfolk who had been called to the services.

The Union Pacific public relations man interested the women's department of *The Salt Lake Tribune* in a feature on "Women in Railroading." Several sweet girl reporters, experienced mainly in the essentials of a wedding story, and the PR man went to the railroad's North yards to talk with women coach cleaners, women carmen or "car toads," and other women laborers.

The PR man had to lead the interviewing and naturally developed the patriotic angle. In response to "And where is your husband?" Mrs. Flo Christiansen answered proudly, "My Nels is in the Navy." So the gamut of the services ran: the Army, the Marine Corps, the Air Corps, the Coast Guard.

All went swimmingly until one interviewee looked the PR man squarely in the eye and when asked for the whereabouts of her husband, declared flatly: "I'd like to know where the son-of-a-bitch is myself."

That broad shoulder for weeping

The late Paul Cowles, superintendent of the western division of the Associated Press, was a kindly man, but he could be irascible when pressed.

One of his subordinates, who filed the north-south wire out of the San Francisco bureau, had been married five times and naturally was having trouble with the fifth. He made it a ritual each morning to update his boss on the latest troubles in the Jones family.

Mr. Cowles suffered through these agonies for six months and nine days before the inevitable explosion came:

"Mr. Jones, your marital problems concern me only insofar as they affect your work. And, Mr. Jones, since your marital problems *do* affect your work adversely, Mr. Jones, *you are fired!*"

PUBLIC UTILITIES: THEIR FEEDING AND CARE

There was a considerable period in which public utilities, particularly railroads and electric companies, were top hands on the American economic ranch, but they now have been under-hounds for a quarter-century. Their competitors, heavily subsidized at the taxpayer's expense, will not allow sins long grown cold to be forgotten. The statute of limitations does run for every offense except murder. And utility mistakes of the 1920's might well be condoned in the 1960's, but they still are flaunted whenever a hoof seems at all likely to slide from the public trough.

In any event, utility operators are in constant need of their senses of humor. Most of them have not lost the required touch. These examples could be multiplied.

Emily Post at work in Butte

When Frank W. Bird was president of the Montana Power Company, Leland Olds, then Chairman of the Federal Power Commission, came out to Butte to negotiate with him. Olds consistently addressed Bird as, "Mr. President." Frank was amused, but he said to me, "Janx, I like that. That's what I'm going to be called. And I'll start with Jimmie, the office boy."

Some days later I asked about the experiment. "Sorry, but it's not in the cards," he reported. "Jimmie came to me yesterday and said, 'I've tried. I really tried. But Goddlemighty, Frank, I just can't do it!'"

What was that spade's name?

The late C. W. Charske, a widely-known railway executive, was an auditor, brought up in the road's accounting department, where there was rigid adherence to that "keen unscrupulous course which knows no doubt, which feels no fear." He was meticulous in dress, in action, and in speech. He called a spade a spade; that is until he fell over one in the back yard of his home at Darien, Connecticut.

Gentle words and kindly

This one has been told from time to time throughout the country, but it probably was related first in 1921 by Stoddard King, columnist for the Spokane *Spokesman Review,* author of the lyrics of "The Long, Long Trail," and writer of light verse which compared favorably with F. P. A.'s.

The Washington Water Power Company had been informed by several indignant customers that one of its linemen had used language so fearsomely sulphurous that it had cast a blue pall over the entire Inland Empire and had withered tomato vines as far away as Moscow, Idaho.

Of course a written report was demanded. Presented on the back of an easement form, it read:

> I and James Rafterskill was repairing a leaky transformer on pole No. 1196 back of 214 North Sprague Street on Tuesday last. Mr. Rafterskill was up on the pole working on that transformer with hot solder metal and he dropped some of that hot solder metal down my neck. So I looked up at him and I said, "James, you really should be more careful."

Do you know your train crew?

The traditional railroad crew is composed of one swell-head (conductor), one hog-head (engineer), one fat-head (fireman), and two pin-heads (brakemen), all directly responsible to a big-belly (division superintendent). Railroad management now seems determined to excise most fat-heads and perhaps a pin-head here and there. The overall national loss, if accompanied by appropriate job-training, just *could* be minimal.

Should she have called the Archbishop of Titipu?

Half-a-century back, the public utility poobah of Scranton, Pennsylvania, was one Major Scranton, an ancestor of that commonwealth's present governor. All complaints about utility service went to the major and he normally dealt with them cheerfully and efficiently.

He was annoyed, however, when he was turned out of bed at 2:30 the morning of March 2, 1905, to be greeted by an anguished female voice: "Major Scranton, Major Scranton, I would have you know that a live eel has just come through my water pipe!"

"Well, madam," he replied crisply, "what the Hell do you expect? Brook trout?"

This also is free-enterprise

John S. Wise relates this adventure of a crew which had undertaken the electrical thawing of frozen water pipes in Allentown, Pennsylvania. Jim Thornbush, as foreman, made all arrangements and did the collecting, while Nels Gramlin operated the electrical equipment.

All went well until the tight-fisted proprietor of a delicatessen objected violently to Jim's standard tariff. The argument was concluded only when

Jim shouted, "Hey, Nels. This damn' dutchman won't pay. Reverse the current and freeze the son-of-a-bitch up again."

Calm, cool, collected, serene

In Kingsport, Tennessee, a meeting of utility employees was held for the express purpose of dealing with automobile accidents. Each operator of a vehicle who found himself in trouble was to remain unemotional and serene, was to refrain from any abuse and, most importantly, was to obtain at once the names and addresses of potential witnesses.

The next day, Bill Wilber was proceeding down the city's main street when a reckless driver turned blindly into that thoroughfare and cauliflowered the left rear fender of Bill's car.

Two citizens who obviously had seen what had happened were standing at the corner. Bill therefore leaped out to approach them, remaining cool, calm, restrained and collected.

"Say," he asked loudly, "Say! Did you two sons-of-bitches see what that gentleman done to me?"

"The creature madly climbing back into its chrysalis"

Every community has its convinced reactionary, the disgruntled butterfly who had preferred his caterpillar existence, who would eagerly have crawled back into his chrysalis. Such a citizen was Sidney Knacklesbrough of Scranton, Pennsylvania, who denounced all innovation, who strongly preferred horse cars and gas street lighting, who paid earnest tribute to what he persisted in calling the "hal-i-kon" era.

This quatrain finally gave Sid substantial pause:
>Here's to the good old halikon days,
>When Scranton was lit by gas,
>When the trip to town took an hour and a half
>And the view was a horse's ass.

Not necessarily from an expert

The late George M. Gadsby of Salt Lake City was stopped on Main Street by a panhandler who asked for a dollar.

"Look, my friend," said Gadsby, "you are trying for entirely too much. If you asked for a dime, or even a quarter, you would get some customers, but a dollar is badly out of line."

"What is *your* name and what do *you* do?"

"I am George Gadsby and I am president of the Utah Power & Light Company."

"Well, I'll tell you, Mr. Gadsby: You run your business and damn' well let me run mine."

That old "high ball" sign

Mrs. Ansel McCrombie, mother of the then president of the Union Pacific Railroad, was about to board that carrier's "Portland Rose" at Omaha when she saw the train's conductor give its engineer the usual on-your-way, or "high ball," signal. "And what, sir," she asked, "does that waving of your arm signify?"

"Aw," said the conductor sourly, "it means get th' Hell outa here!"

Several hours later, the conductor learned Mrs. McCrombie's identity and he came back to her exuding apologies: "I *am* distressed, Madam. I *do* regret my rudeness. Our baby had the colic last night, etc., etc."

Mrs. McCrombie listened pleasantly and smilingly. But she did not speak. She gave the "high ball" sign.

Antelope Frank

We were in the deep doldrums of 1932.
Frank Kerr, then president of the Montana

Power Company, in attendance at a New York gathering of utility executives, was asked whether he could report that his enterprise was even holding its own.

"I can give you the picture best," said Kerr, "by telling you one from my own early 20's, when I was probably the fastest man west of the Rocky Mountains. Nobody would bet against me even before this happened, but from that time on, everybody called me 'Antelope Frank'.

"I was riding across country from Great Falls to Billings one March night and was dozing in the saddle when my horse stepped in a chuck hole, stumbled, threw me and ran away. There I was: no food, no water; and fifty miles from anywhere. I walked as far as I could, but finally dropped, completely worn out, and went to sleep when I hit the ground.

"It was cold when I opened my eyes just before sun-up. There was a big, buck antelope snuggled up to me for warmth. His legs were under him, but his tail was up, so his tokus was winkin' at me, within a foot of my right hand.

"I knew he would jump the minute I moved, but I thought that if I could somehow hook him, my life would be saved. I gathered myself without twitchin' a muscle and made my move. Well, my aim was true, right on the target, but he took off with me."

The narrator paused and an impatient listener asked, "All right! What happened? What happened?"

Frank sighed before he answered. "I run him even for a mile and a half, but I never could gain quite enough to crook my finger!"

Mother milked by the light of the moon

Clyde Ellis, former Arkansas Congressman and now Executive Secretary of the National Rural Cooperatives Association, has consistently appeared in behalf of public power projects.

One Congressional hearing involved a Southwestern Power Administration request for millions of dollars for steam power plants and transmission lines. In this instance, Clyde's principal opponent was C. Hamilton Moses, president of Arkansas Power & Light Company and its long-time counsel, who was called upon after Clyde had delivered substantially this peroration: "In my early days, I lived on a little hill farm in the Ozark Mountains in Arkansas. Many nights I saw my poor, dear mother milking cows by the light of the moon. And I took a solemn oath that I would bend my heart and strength, even in the halls of Congress, to get electricity out to these farms so that no other boy's mother would ever have to milk her cows by the light of the moon."

Moses replied: "I have long known former Congressman Clyde Ellis and I have watched his great accomplishments with pride. I realize how persuasive is his milking-cows-by-the-light-of-the-moon argument before this committee. I am, however, a little at a loss. There were eight Ellis boys—all growing up to be splendid citizens under the influence of a fine mother and father. I lived on a farm, too, even though my mother had only three boys. But *she* never had to milk cows in the moonlight. While that fine, devoted mother, raising her eight children in those Ozark Hills, was milking cows by the light of the moon, I wonder what Clyde Ellis and his seven brothers were doing. You know, Cyde, I don't believe I would ever sob that story again."

He didn't.

Who remembers "car cards"?

Jake Heckma of the old Commonwealth & Southern Company told about a banking institution in Grand Rapids, Michigan (let's call it the "Ninth National"), which had its difficulties. One of its assistant cashiers extracted $150,000 and departed; the cashier purloined $385,000 and left the bloodhounds baffled; and finally the president escaped, with $1,064,000 and a blonde, to one of the

Latin American countries with which we then had no extradition treaty.

Ninth National's public image suffered. Deposits sank abysmally. Something had to be done. Advertising naturally was undertaken and car cards on the community's then street railway lines were among the media used.

This was the bank's triumphant effort:

THE NINTH NATIONAL BANK OF
GRAND RAPIDS, MICHIGAN
CAPITAL AND SURPLUS, $646,900
COURTEOUS, FRIENDLY, FOLKSY
THE BANK WITH THE HELPING
HAND

Technique among the Rockies

Frank Kerr of Butte, Montana, had just extracted a valuable franchise from a group of particularly recalcitrant county commissioners and I asked for his technique. "Janx, my boy," he answered, "I just *ain'ted* the sons-of-bitches to death!"

Boss of the ranch

On a Saturday afternoon in the long-ago days when Electric Bond and Share Company was a subsidiary of General Electric Company, S. Z. Mitchell, the tyrant of Bond and Share, had taken more than his share of telephone calls, including two from C. A. Coffin, Chairman of the Board of General Electric. S. Z. therefore called in his secretary, Walter Schweikhardt, and declared, "Walter, you are not to put through a single 'phone call the rest of the day. I won't even talk to God Almighty or the Pope."

Some ten minutes later, Schweikhardt appeared to say, "Telephone, Mr. Mitchell."

"Goddamit, Walter, didn't I say I wouldn't even talk to God Almighty or the Pope?"

"Yessir, Mr. Mitchell. Mr. Coffin's on the 'phone."

Mitchell grunted and reached.

As Schweikhardt and his assistant, Joe Damblos, who was a devout Catholic, left the office, Joe observed privately, "Walter, Mr. Mitchell shouldn't have said that. He shouldn't have said that about the Pope!"

Ask the directors

In the late '30's, Kinsey M. Robinson, then President of the Washington Water Power Company, was on the stand for cross-examination by a public-power lawyer who, having collected no tittle of change, asked sourly, "Mr. Robinson, do you mean to sit there and say that you really believe you are worth $40,000 a year?"

"No," Kinsey replied gently, "I don't. But my directors do and who am I to question their judgment?"

The consonant does differ

In the remote 1920's, Pacific Telephone & Telegraph Company was in the middle of an important rate case. Public interest had been aroused, so the proceeding was held in the Portland city council chambers.

The company's venerable and bewhiskered chief engineer was on the stand when a countryman from the Coos Bay area came in, noticed several attractive telephone operators on the front row, and asked a neighbor what it was all about.

"Why didn't you know, my friend? This is a rate case."

"A rape case! Good God! Is that old feller the dee-fendant and is all them gals the prosecutrixes?"

The gentle bouncer

For a large part of the 1940's, the Securities and Exchange Commission maintained its offices in Philadelphia's Penn Athletic Club Building. Its staff worked hard, as did the representatives of litigants, and from time to time relaxation was had at a night club called Waldron's.

This particular evening, a group at the night club included Dick Bronwyn, Commission trial examiner. A positive person, Dick was so disenchanted with the monologuist filling in as the chorus changed costumes that he began to shout loudly, "Call the next case! By God, call the next case!"

And he was attracting undue attention when Paul Waldron, proprietor of the establishment and a former heavyweight wrestler who did his own bouncing, decided to take a hand. Paul tapped Dick on the shoulder and said sharply, "Listen, mister, you're an important executive of one of this country's major enterprises. You're making a fool of yourself and you're hurting yourself and your company. Now I don't want to hear one more word out of you!"

Dick straightened up, squared his shoulders and beamed around the room. He was a good boy the rest of the evening.

Agony down to the toes

In 1931, when depression was heavy on the land, I participated in a proceeding before the public utilities commission of one of the smaller states. Its members were paid $10 per diem for attendance at sessions and they were grateful.

One such brother, a farmer by long practice, was distressed by the highly technical character of depreciation testimony we were presenting. He protested to me at the first morning recess, "Look, Mr. Gussman, why does all this stuff of yours have to be damn' dusty. It makes me ache down to my toes. 'Fo' God, Mistah Gussman, I'd rather plow!"

THE GREAT EMPTY SPACES

These are from the far West, excluding Los Angeles and its environs, known throughout prohibition as "Bevo Junction" (one of the St. Louis breweries was attempting to peddle a near-beer called Bevo; it was slop). The aroma of Paul Bunyan and his mighty Babe, the Blue Ox, will reach some nostrils.

Idaho's Pun'kin Valley Line

One of my good friends was Hyrum E. Dunn, who built the Payette Valley Railroad in Idaho. Known colloquially as the Pun'kin Valley Line, it ran 28 miles from Payette to Emmett.

In his promotion of the Payette-Emmett area, Dunn printed vivid and imaginative posters, one of which declared:

"If I could sell my New York interests, I would settle in the Payette Valley."
(Signed) Lydia E. Pinkham.

For the edification of younger readers, gynecologists of the late 19th and early 20th centuries looked with jaundiced eyes on the well-advertised compound of this lady. Her beloved elixir, so stoutly and satisfyingly alcoholic, was described as "a boon to womankind," offered out of Mrs. Pinkham's "love for the human race."

When a community cooperated

The Payette Valley Railroad, pretty much built on a shoestring by Hyrum E. Dunn, was absorbed in 1914 by the Oregon Short Line, now part of the Union Pacific.

The Payette Valley's one locomotive was deadheaded into Salt Lake City for possible rehabilitation. Timing his message with the arrival of the engine, Dunn sent this telegram to W. H. Bancroft, general manager of the Oregon Short Line:

"Please return whistle on Engine 505. I borrowed it from the Troy Steam Laundry."

Strictly for business purposes

Hyrum Dunn observed the amenities. He also knew that secretaries grew up to be general managers in the railroading of the early 20th century.

Payette Valley produced excellent cider and Dunn wanted to present a keg to W. H. Bancroft, general manager of the Oregon Short Line. He had access to the railroad telegraph system, but messages were confined to business purposes.

Dunn solved this problem by sending the following telegram before he shipped not one but *two* kegs of cider to Fred H. Knickerbocker, then secretary to Bancroft and later a major railroad executive:

"C.Ider and brother on Train 5 date."

When recommendations flamed

Hyrum Dunn once asked a Salt Lake City friend to give his nephew a job.

"Why, certainly, Hy. What can the boy do?"

"We-l-l, he shoots a good game of pool."

The admiral and the sliding pie

Mrs. Walter Holt of California was entertaining a bemedalled admiral just after World War II began. Under the skeptical eye of her Chinese cook, she had prepared a graham-cracker apple pie and all went well until that succulent was put on the table. Unfortunately, it had been served on a glass plate and as Mrs. Holt attempted to cut portions, it skidded and slid, defying all her efforts. The Chinese cook perspired, averted his gaze and, finally deciding that he had lost enough face, exclaimed, "*She* make this pie! I make good pie!"

Not for export to Hollywood

Claude Engberg, president of the Pioneer Baseball league, returned to his home town of Scipio, Utah, and conferred with the hamlet's lone gas station attendant for the latest on what was going on in the community.

"Yeh, that pretty little Mary Ellen Jones finally married that big lug of a Prentice boy," said Claude's informant. "And is he ugly! Why he's so ugly he looks just like a calcimined horny toad."

Are you a philosopher and friend?

There is the "guide, friend and mentor" who likes to point out to fellow travelers on a crack transcontinental train the antelopes of Wyoming in the vicinity of Laramie and Medicine Bow. He then makes the authoritative statement that Jackelopes, a cross between the antelope and the big buck jackrabbit, are the fastest things on four feet. And rare animals indeed, because they breed only during a flash of lightning.

Ebenezer and Bryce Canyon

One of the better treatments of "dudes," or visitors, involves leading the uninitiated to the brim of Bryce Canyon, in southern Utah. Let him surrender to the breath-taking beauty of nature's fantasy, and then tell him the story of the naming of the canyon—the only national park named for an individual.

Bryce Canyon National Park is named for Ebenezer Bryce, who settled briefly in this scenic wonderland. He was a pioneer with restless feet, always seeking that greener pasture over the next divide.

When Bryce Canyon was first designated a national monument, Ebenezer had gone on to distant parts, but an enterprising reporter sought him out for reaction to this perpetuation of his name.

The old man said with a straight face and simple sincerity:

"I do remember that canyon somewhat—it was a helluva place to lose a cow."

Look out for him

The Hallarwi Indians of northwestern Utah had a problem of succession which is still interesting. The Chief had twin sons with equal and identical rights to succeed him. To deal with this duality, the tribal council decreed that the young man who brought back the most unusual game would be the next chief.

The brothers, Flying Arrow and Falling Rocks, loved each other as brothers should, but the decree had to be followed. Flying Arrow came back in three days with a white buffalo, but the days turned into weeks and the weeks into months and Falling Rocks did not return. Reluctantly Flying Arrow became chief on the death of his father, but he made it clear that if Falling Rocks returned with more unusual game, he would be chief. And Flying Arrow ordered a continuous search for his missing brother.

That is the reason to this day for the many signs in the West which read:

"Look out for Falling Rocks."

There is a sequel. Only recently the *Spokesman-Review* of Spokane, Washington, used the head "Falling Rocks kills North Idaho Miner." The purists assert that this use of the singular verb is proof positive that Falling Rocks is now in the Shoshone county jail at Kellogg, Idaho.

Babe, the Blue Ox, pulled their tents

Once upon a time the Hallarwi Indians operated in the northwest section of Utah. Nomadic and nocturnal, they traveled at night, made a new camp in the pre-dawn darkness and slept until dusk. They derived their name from the tribe's sunset ritual. When the Hallarwi chief awakened, he pulled aside the flap of his tepee, and asked:

"Where the Hallarwi?"

Wagoneering in Nevada

Gib Berry, Kentucky native who wrought a name for himself as a western mining engineer, made friends easily.

One of them, a chronic alcoholic, greeted him gaily in Ely, Nevada with, "Congratulate me, Gib, I'm on the wagon!"

"That's fine, Fitz, just fine. How long has this been going on?"

"W-e-l-l, day after tomorrow, it'll be two days."

Trenchermen, a vanishing race

Judge Barkwell, one of the West's better trenchermen, opened his day with a waterglass full of bourbon.

His breakfast consisted of a large orange juice, fruit in season, such as a whole cantaloupe or eighteen (no-more-no-less) stewed prunes, ham or sausage and five eggs, fifteen pancakes with syrup and butter, and ample coffee.

A physical examination finally became necessary and the judge reported truthfully on his breakfast intake.

Telling a friend of the physical examination and his honest report on that normal breakfast, the good judge made this candid reply to the friend's startled inquiry, "For God's sake, what did the doctor think?":

"Well, he thought it was a-plenty."

The man meant what he said

Bud Rogers stumbled over a large black dog as he emerged from the revolving door of Boise, Idaho's old Chamber of Commerce building. He aimed a hearty kick at the animal, shouting, "Get outa here, you black son-of-a-bitch!" Then he turned to see that he had been followed by the venerable Bishop Glorieux of the Catholic diocese of Idaho. "I do apologize, Bishop," said Bud contritely. But the Bishop replied, "Think nothing of it, my son. That is the first time in a long life that I ever heard that characterization applied correctly."

Speed among the white pines

There are few phenomena more terrifying than what is known as the "crown" fire that sometimes sweeps through the tops of dry trees at speeds up to 30 miles an hour, destroying and devastating as it goes. In the early 1920's, northern Idaho had been experiencing a series of particularly disastrous forest fires and all available man power was being pressed into service, including in the case of one crew a ribbon clerk recruited in Spokane, Washington.

The young man held up reasonably well until he came face to face with a shocking, wind-driven, crown fire. After one look, he rushed into camp, gathered his few belongings and started down the road at top speed. He certainly hoped that he was moving in the direction of Spokane, but he was at least sure that he was getting away from the inferno.

Sam Hendron, the crew's foreman, saw Arthur Brandol, camp cook, the next day. "Art, how about that Spokane feller?" he asked. "Was he runnin' when he left the fire?"

"Naw, Sam. It wasn't runnin'. You couldn't exactly call it runnin'. He was just puttin' one foot down once in a while to steer with!"

Service de luxe

Forty-five years back, when this happened, the town of Whitebird, in central Idaho, was splendidly isolated. No telephones, no radio, not even a telegraph line, and a road which gave pause even to the most robust Model T. Southern Idaho was on Mountain Time, northern Idaho on Pacific, but in Whitebird, as one of its leading citizens reported to me, "We just kinda go on a time of our own."

When Russell Cunningham, forest supervisor for the area, brought his Connecticut bride to Whitebird for the first time, he told Joe Varneed, proprietor of the hotel, that she was an Easterner, not fully accustomed to establishments in Western communities. He therefore asked Joe to make an unusual effort in her behalf.

"I gotcha, Russ," Joe replied. "I'll take care of you." And spotting the institution's sole chambermaid, he called out, "Hey, Nellie! Fix up Number 6. Fix 'er up good. Change the sheets and everything!"

Recalcitrance in Montana

Frank Kerr of Butte used to tell about a transcontinental mule train that stopped in Havre, Montana, so that its passengers could be watered. When efforts were made to reload, one peculiarly obdurate citizen planted his feet and refused to move. Tugging, hauling, pushing, beating and tail-twisting had all been tried to no avail. Of course the train crew had assembled to watch the performance. Then a countryman stepped up and gave the mule a tremendous kick in the belly. That recalcitrant broke wind prodigiously and climbed up the loading ramp. One of the brakemen turned to his partner: "Hell, Pete, I didn't realize that the son-of-a-bitch had his air-brakes set."

The spectator unfascinated

Frank W. Bird of Montana knew a mountaineer who came around a bend in the rugged path leading to his log cabin home to find his wife engaged in a life-and-death struggle with a grizzly bear. "Hm-m-m," observed the ardent husband. "Never saw a fight I was less interested in!"

"Not before I built Grand Coulee"

Guy Atkinson, a great California builder whose appearance was less impressive than his performance, had undertaken to construct a number of ocean-going ships soon after we entered World War II. His qualifications were being inquired into at a hearing called for that and related purposes and he was under cross-examination by a youthful government lawyer.

"But Mr. Atkinson, it is true that you never have built ships before, isn't it?"

"Yes, that's right. And it also is true that I never had built a dam before I built Grand Coulee."

"Come, come, Mr. Atkinson, what really makes you think that you will be able to build these ships?"

"Listen, sonny! Anything anybody can draw plans for I can build!"

THE MEDICAL FRATERNITY

Among those who take themselves with earnest seriousness, physicians rank only slightly below ministers and politicians. They have substantial justification, because they are required each day to deal with life and death, as well as socialized medicine. Their humor is often intra-professional, esoteric, not for laymen. It can also be a shade grisly, as can be testified by any woman medical student who ever has found a severed thumb in the pocket of her gown. But the boys have acute and perceptive risibilities. The few specimens here offered must be surpassed every morning at Johns Hopkins or at the Mayo Clinic.

Has obstetrics any future?

William Tuttle, from the hills west of Asheville, North Carolina, was in his third year of medicine at Chapel Hill. Home for a brief visit, he naturally was questioned about his courses, and his father asked what he expected his specialty to be.

"Well, dad, I have given it a lot of thought and I have finally decided to specialize in obstetrics. That branch of medicine is important; it will let me give great service. I am going to surrender my life to it."

"Sorry, son, but you're wastin' your time.

You're goin' to study it. You're goin' to work on it. You're goin' to learn everything they is to know about it. And then some damn' fool is goin' to come up with a cure for it and you're goin' to be out of luck!"

An oculist in retirement

When Dr. John J. McFord, eminent and warmly liked oculist, retired from the practice at age 70, his many friends decided that a testimonial was in order. Funds were collected, what seemed an appropriate gift was made ready, and the doctor was guest of honor at a community banquet.

The memorial presented at the evening's climax was a large and handsome replica of the human eye, its pupil a splendid portrait of the good doctor.

Dr. McFord responded, "My dear friends, I am profoundly indebted to you for this demonstration of your interest and affection. Let me say that I am especially grateful on two counts: first, for your kindliness and generosity, and, second, for the happy circumstance that I am not a proctologist!"

When parking tickets were new

Even when automobiles were new and rare, medical men operated them. Dr. William Lee

Smith, of Boise, Idaho, who owned one, had parked in a strictly forbidden area. Just as he returned to his car, a policeman was preparing one of the primordial traffic tickets. Dr. Smith called attention to the caduceus on his car's radiator and explained that his profession gave him unusual privileges.

The officer listened respectfully, put away his pencil and replied, "Beg y' pardon. It's all right, pal. You docs is exemplified!"

Name your target, pal

Dr. Charles Mayo of the celebrated clinic which bears his name was stopped by a prospective patient who inquired, "Sir, are you the head doctor?"

"Naw," answered Dr. Charley. "I'm the belly doctor!"

That original honeymoon

I sometimes think I can laugh at myself. In any event, I observed to my surgeon after extensive thoracic whittling which involved the removal of one rib and the separating of two others, "Doc, I just want to tell you that if the Lord caused Adam as much pain when He created Eve as I have had since you worked me over, it must have been a helluva honeymoon."

Hospital laughter; and tears

Some years ago, after an operation for the excision of much of my left lung, I was trying to rest in a New York hospital room when I received a letter from Pierce Butler, Jr.

"I was delighted to hear that you are getting along so nicely, Janx," he said in part. "But I want you to know that I had an old friend in just your case who seemed to be making satisfactory progress when he took a sudden turn for the nurse."

I laughed and then wanted to cry. *Please* don't make 'em even *smile* when the thoracic cavity or even the *sphinctus ani* has been subjected to surgery.

Togetherness in the hospital

George Blandmore's nurse in a Salt Lake City hospital was a devoted apostle of "togetherness": "Now we'll take *our* pill"; "It's time for *our* enema"; "Please turn over so we can rub *our* back"; and much more.

George was fed to the tonsils and opportunity came when his nurse brought in both breakfast and a specimen bottle. "We'll eat all of *our* breakfast," she said. "And then we will take *our* specimen."

Apple juice had been served that morning and when the nurse left him alone briefly, George poured it into the specimen bottle.

"My, my!" she said when she returned. "Our specimen *is* cloudy this morning, isn't it?"

George took the bottle.

"By God, it is cloudy at that," he said. "Let's give it a re-run."

He tossed off the apple juice; his nurse ran screaming down the hall; and George went home that afternoon.

Two of what?

Clem Holding of North Carolina, who served in World War I and therefore is no longer a boy, says, "With modern medicine doing so well at increasing life expectancy, we had better be careful about expanding the national debt any further—we might have to pay it off ourselves. In all events, I am inclined to believe that the condition of a man can best be judged by what he takes two of: stairs or pills."

Poultice for the doctor

Let's call him Dr. Norman Younkler, a distinguished urologist and rampant showman who took particular delight in shocking audiences large or small with vivid and sanguinary accounts of his operations.

On this occasion, according to a veteran of the Virginia School of Medicine, Dr. Younkler was in the process of being initiated into Alpha Omega Alpha, honorary medical society which had been formed after Younkler's student days. The ceremony was under way and one Vergil Blade, the young man in charge, was reciting some of the society's idealistic precepts when Dr. Younkler interrupted him. "My friend," declared the doctor, "I can't allow myself to be initiated into this estimable organization. I am not worthy of it! I do not deserve the honor!" Then Younkler recited the full and gory circumstances of an abortion which he, as a youthful intern, had performed, in his apartment, on the person of an unlucky Oklahoma cousin. "You see," he concluded, "I don't belong. We cannot continue with this ritual."

Mr. Blade took a deep breath before he replied, "Doctor, I think I see a way out of this dilemma. If you will solemnly promise us here and now that you won't do it again, I believe we can go ahead!"

It was Dr. Younkler's turn to be startled. All the drama was being drained out of his confession. He gulped, promised and became a member of Alpha Omega Alpha.

PRE-EPILOGUE AND EP.

Harvey Hannah, chairman of the Tennessee Public Utilities Commission more than a generation ago, had a Louisiana friend who possessed that area's most remarkable bull, Horace Quintillus. Horace's boss, McGammon McGowen, owned a large farm which bordered the main line of the Southern Pacific for a mile and it was the bull's habit to meet that railroad's top passenger train at the eastern boundary of the place and race it for that measured mile. Horace invariably won.

McGowen would have been less than human if he had not boasted about Horace. The word got around. At last a delegation of skeptical friends came out from town on a Wednesday morning to inspect the bull and see him in action.

Old Mac spotted these friends as they approached his large home. He knew intuitively what they had in mind and went into a hurried conference with Henry O'Mallieu, his foreman and strong right arm. "That gang has come to look at Horace," he said. "I can smell it. Get rid of 'em. I don't care what you say or do. I'm on my way to the attic."

The front door bell rang, long and loudly. After appropriate deliberation, a smiling, cordial and urbane Henry appeared: "Good mornin'! What can I do for you gentlemen?"

"You can guess why we're here. We want to talk to Mac and we want that famous bull put through his paces. Where is the old boy?"

"So sorry, gentlemen, but Mr. Mac left this mornin' fo' Atlanta and fo' other most important places."

"Where's he goin'?"

"Well, after Atlanta, he takes off for New York City, then Boston up in Yankee land, then them Twin Cities out in Minnesota, then Memphis and on home."

"When will he be back?"

"Hm-m-m. I'm countin' up. This is Wednesday mornin' and he'll be right here again Friday evenin'. That's day after tomorrow."

"Nonsense! Crazy nonsense! Are you tryin' to tell us that he's gonna cover all that country in just two days?"

"Yes, suh! Yes, suh! He's goin' all them places and he be back home Friday evenin'. Y'see, suh, he's a-ridin' his bull!"

As Frank Bird of Montana would say at this point, the time has come to obscenity on the fire, call the dog and go home. There are those who prefer to call the dog first. Herman Phleger, ornament of the San Francisco bar, is of that persuasion. The reader may take his choice.

THE DECALOGUE OF THE HUMOROUS ANECDOTE

Few, all, all too few, of our cherished fellow citizens know how to tell a story for the purpose of dissipating tension, of exercising the ventral and thoracic cavities. Most of them ordinarily don't know whether the story is funny. Furthermore, they labor it. Their tarnished bespanglings impede its movement. They prolong it without purpose. They have neither taste nor talent.

They are hideously without a sense of appositeness. Several years ago, I offered to a male banquet group the decalogue which is to follow, fleshing it out with many of the yarns in my collection. I was followed by the president of a substantial business enterprise and the president of a large engineering college. Each of them said, in effect, "I am sorry that I have to violate your rules, Janx, but I think the boys will be interested in this one."

Then each repeated a single anecdote: ancient, grimy, bewhiskered, crassly vulgar, utterly without relevance to any current observations; not funny. Each knew that he was to speak at a stag party and each had dredged up one story. Even I, Old Blushless Janx, colored slightly, my emotions compounded equally of exacerbation, pity, sympathy and nausea. Can't the business statesman, the college executive, remember three or four reasonably appropriate yarns and then learn how to tell them decently? There are engaging exceptions, but for most speakers there should be a law. On second thought, not a law. It would be no more enforceable than the Volstead Act. Conspicuous hangings in various parts of the country would better serve the public interest.

This decalogue, prepared with my assistance and under my supervision, attempts to provide instruction of sorts. The author's consent to its publication was given grudgingly. It is my experience that, in such circumstances, the most effective hold is the hammerlock.

In all events, here are the commandments. They represent the summation of much trial and error, success and failure, roaring laughter and the dull squash of a mature egg. Persons who memorize these admonitions and will forward an affidavit to that effect to my Charlottesville address will receive a valuable certificate, engraved on honeysuckle parchment, with effluence of dogwood.

> *No. 1. Be brief. Some ornamentation is legitimate, but it must not impede the movement of the story. Get to the point. Promptly!*

That one could hardly be more obvious. If you string 'em out, you will bore, then lose, your audience. At least, unless you are a poet of parts. And you, pal, don't quite qualify.

No. 2. Begin, if you can, with a self-deprecatory yarn. Nothing quite so quickly wins the sympathy of an audience as a story at the speaker's expense. The basic ingredient of a sense of humor is the ability to laugh at one's self.

Think of the speakers who have employed this opening successfully. The great Henry Watterson, for example, used to begin one of his famous lectures by saying: "Ladies and gentlemen, my subject tonight will be 'Money and Morals'. Having none of either, I feel abundantly qualified to discuss both!" Joel Priest launched many a successful talk with his Sam Jones experience and others in my collection are of this same category. Think of your most deeply embarrassing, humiliating experience and then relate it smilingly. They will love you from Pocatello, Idaho, to Pompton Beach, Florida.

No. 3. Never tell a story which does not involve some element of surprise. If the point of the gag is obvious, if it is "telegraphed" in the first sentence or two, the tale is not worth the telling. You must in effect play a practical joke on your hearers, leading their minds in one direction and then suddenly reversing your course.

If you will parse just a few sound stories, this caveat will seem a rule of nature. Max Eastman has elaborated the theory persuasively in his "Enjoyment of Laughter."

How often you have squirmed from lobe to lobe when an un-punch line loomed unmistakably on the horizon and the speaker blabbered blitheringly along. If only a hard roll, flung accurately, were a deadly weapon!

> *No. 4. Never tell a maculate yarn unless the humor is strong enough to carry the dirt easily and lightly. Smut for smut's sake is offensive even in a Bowery bar room.*

The thoroughly dirty story is ordinarily the product of a curdled mind. It is filthy without being funny. Its purpose ordinarily is to shock rather than to amuse.

Whether the humor *can* carry the dirt obviously is a matter of judgment and the more tender-minded will not agree with the tougher. Much plainly depends upon the character of your audience. *And* the common sense of individual auditors. I once told a tale which seemed legitimate to me, as it does to most males, but which was not for women and children. Sadly enough, one listener's fiancée was my daughter's roommate at Wellesley. And she got the story from the pale-gray young jackass who was to marry her. My daughter's letter to me might have been more bristling, but I don't know how.

>   *No. 5. Never try to clean up or expurgate a story which is tinctured with vulgarity but which is, nevertheless, genuinely humorous. All too often, when you clean 'em up, they just aren't funny any more.*

In the early 1920's, Fisher Muldrow told my friend Ridney Walworth a story which involved Bill Hargiss, who then coached football at Kansas. Fisher and Rid were having a drink at the bar of a Great Lakes cruise ship when the tale was related and Rid was so delighted that he beat a new Panama hat to death.

Paula, Rid's wife, had observed the episode, but she did not hear the tale. She demanded and demanded it and finally, after nine years, seven months and twenty-one days, Rid told it to her in a cleaned-up, bowdlerized, expurgated version.

Paula looked Rid between the eyes and observed sternly, "I don't see anything amusing about that!"

He wiped the perspiration from his steaming brow and replied, "My dear, neither do I!"

I have told the original on various occasions, each time offering $50 to anybody who could launder it effectively and keep it funny. No takers!

No, the yarn is not in this collection. Let's just say that I'm a liberal, but an *old* liberal.

But I *have* told several of the specimens published in this volume and have scoured away the grime, such as it is. In each instance, the laughter was hardly polite.

Use a detergent on 'em and they aren't funny. Did you ever try to eat un-salted oatmeal?

> *No. 6. Never tell a dialect story unless you are completely at home in that dialect.* **Did you ever hear a bona fide New England Yankee, fully equipped with nasal twang, attempt a negro story? Child birth may be a more painful experience, but *I* have my doubts.**

Dialect stories (*i.e.,* yarns that depend primarily on dialect) are plainly on their way out, for dialects themselves are disappearing. Education, radio, television are mighty forces. Their jargons often leave much to be desired, but they plainly are suppressing dialects. Then, too, the dialect yarn categorizes, which almost always is offensive.

In any event, dialect *is* agonizing unless it is handled with easy familiarity. Any straining is painful and therefore dissipates the sense of "being in fun."

> *No. 7. Never tell a merely fabricated story— most sheer smut falls in that category. The only anecdotes worth repeating are those that actually have happened or*

> *which, without putting too much strain on the elasticity of a man's fancy, might have happened.*

Smut is concocted. The tellable tale almost always involves either a specific event or a legitimate, factually-inspired flight of the imagination. And even episodes that *have* happened sometimes are not even smoking-room material. It is submitted that the human genitals, male or female, are not *per se* hilarious.

> *No. 8. Never repeat a story unless it has some measure of relevance to the discussion in hand. When the fabled American Common Man says, "Ah, that reminds me!" he is a congenital liar. The fact is that he has been holding his gin-soured breath awaiting any opportunity to tell his only story, a rancid, barnacle-encrusted obscenity which his grandfather failed to sell to the Police Gazette in 1874.*

Appositeness! Relevance! Appropriateness! Some connection, however forced, with the occasion! *Please* don't tell a Pat and Mike tale and then launch a dissertation on light and heavy carbon. If you go after a laugh, arrange for an easy transition to the subject matter of your address. There *is* an episode in your own experience which will provide the bridge. It is important that you dig until you find it.

> *No. 9. Tell the tale as if it has happened to you, or at least in your presence. "Now this is a true story" is the unfailing hallmark of the amateur.*

That celebrated radio inquiry, "Vas you dere, Sharlie?" was heart-warmingly sound humor. The skeptic had not been on hand. He was required to challenge, with nothing more than personal dubiety, the forceful testimony of an eye-witness. He couldn't win. Verisimilitude attracts and holds attention. Use names and dates. Offer, if briefly, a bill of particulars. After all, it's *your* story. "This is a true story!" Ugh! Bush league!

> *No. 10. Don't tell 'em at all, at least unless you observe this Decalogue or similarly restrictive commandments of your own devising.*

Aw, go ahead. If you have read this far, there cannot be the slightest question about your enhanced status. *Somebody* may laugh!